T0040754

Sing **JAZZ!**
Leadsheets For
76 Jazz Vocals

SECOND FLOOR MUSIC

EXCLUSIVELY DISTRIBUTED BY

HAL•LEONARD®
CORPORATION
7777 W. BLUEMOUND RD. P.O. BOX 13819 MILWAUKEE, WI 53213

Editor: Dr. Gloria Cooper
Book Design: Maureen Sickler
Cover Design & Artwork: Terry Chamberlain
Biographies: Zan Stewart
Discography: Dean Pratt & Steve Lambert
Music Engraving: Osho Endo
A DON SICKLER PRODUCTION

INTRODUCTION

Sing JAZZ! contains music composed by some of the world's finest jazz composers and performers. Many of the selections included here were originally instrumental compositions; however, in this volume they appear as songs with lyrics. With its unique emphasis on selections drawn from the astonishingly rich world of instrumental jazz, *Sing JAZZ!* opens up a completely new range of repertoire for the vocalist. Thanks to the talented singers and lyricists who wrote the lyrics in *Sing JAZZ!*, vocalists can now add these songs to their repertoire.

In many cases when lyrics are written by someone other than the composer of the instrumental composition, the song with lyrics is given a new title. The table of contents shows both: the lyricized title (*One Fine Day* by Ray Bryant and lyricist L. Aziza Miller) and the original "instrumentally known as" title (Ray Bryant's *Cubano Chant*). You may not recognize the title *Beloved*, music by Clifford Brown and lyric by Meredith d'Ambrosio; however, the classic instrumental *Daahoud* should be familiar to most. A separate index by instrumental title is included. *Sing JAZZ!* thus provides an opportunity to explore classic jazz material in a new way.

The songs included in this book are in keys for a medium-range voice, comfortable for most medium-range singers.

A helpful hints section includes detailed information on notation, style and form, as well as insights into performance techniques that will help users benefit the most from the leadsheets. The lyrics are shown under the music and are also presented separately, in a "lyrics alone" section. Brief biographies of the artists provide a historical context. Several indexes (by composer, lyricist, original instrumental title, and tempo/style) allow easy access to the material.

Measures are numbered at the beginning of each staff, and rehearsal letters will help in reading and rehearsing the songs. A tempo/rhythmic "feel" indication, such as medium swing, bossa, samba, or ballad, is on each lead sheet. These suggested tempos and styles are often taken from the recorded versions. However, given the individuality of every artist with regard to style, interpretation, nuances, and inflections, feel free to choose your own unique approach.

We encourage you to seek out recorded versions of the compositions in this book. If a song has been recorded with the lyric included here, the vocalist is noted in the table of contents. Also, recording credits are shown on the leadsheets. Additional vocal and instrumental recordings are listed in the discography. If there are no recording credits on the leadsheet, look in the discography to see which instrumental artists have recorded it.

Small group (combo) arrangements are available for some titles, and more are in preparation. Listings of these arrangements appear at the end of this book. You can also request a full catalog from www.secondfloormusic.com (or call 1-800-637-2852).

This folio provides . . .

• the jazz vocalist the opportunity to add fresh new repertoire for performances and recordings.

• a pianist/coach with new repertoire to suggest to singers.

• new song ideas to a choral director looking for something inventive to arrange for a performance.

Regardless of one's specialty or level of expertise, there is a wealth of music to explore and sing in the pages of *Sing JAZZ!*

Dr. Gloria Cooper

Sing JAZZ! *Leadsheets For 76 Jazz Vocals*

Fm

Sung by Kevin Mahogany on Another Time, Another Place (Warner Bros 46699)

Another Time, Another Place

Instrumentally known as "Appointment In Milano"

Music by Robert Watson
Lyric by Pamela Baskin-Watson

* if no Bass, Piano *8vb.*

All My Love, Especially For You

Instrumentally known as "Especially For You . . ."

Music by John Oddo
Lyric by Pamela Baskin-Watson

Slow Light funk

9

Em7♭5

Sung by Carmelita Esposito on The Men I Love (The Family Company 1)

Alone Again

Music and Lyric by
J.R. Monterose

Alone With Just My Dreams

Music and Lyric by
George Duvivier

Ballad

A - lone _____ with just my dreams all else is gone, no - thing left it seems, just

mem - o - ries _____ and haunt - ing mel - o - dies re - main. _____ A -

lone _____ with just my dreams, tears cloud the moon, gone are all its beams. When

stars ap - pear _____ it seems they want to hear your voice _____ once a - gain. Oh,

why did this have to hap - pen? _____ I ask my - self is it true? Is it

fair that I suf - fer so just for fall - ing in love _ with some - one such as you? _____ Why

try _____ to car - ry on? Life's just a shell now that you are gone. Does

1. to solos (1-32)

*fate de - cree _____ that I must al - ways be a - lone _____ with just my dreams? *____ A -*

2. last time

al - ways be a - lone _____ with just my dreams?

* pick-up to melody Ⓐ only

Copyright © 1945 (renewed 1973) TWENTY-EIGHTH STREET MUSIC

Sung by Dena DeRose on Another World (Sharp Nine Records CD 1016)

Another World

Music and Lyric by
Rob Bargad

* pick-up to melody Ⓐ only

Sung by Kenny Hagood on The Bebop Boys (Savoy SJL 2225)

Baby, I'm Coming Home

Music and Lyric by
Chuck Wayne

Cm

Sung by Sheila Jordan on Jazz Child (High Note HCD 7029)

Ballad For Miles

Music and Lyric by
Sheila Jordan

Slow and dreamy

Intro (instrumental)

* Letters in circles indicate bass notes. The rhythmic placement of the (Cm) harmony should vary.
In performance, Ms. Jordan often combines this composition with a ballad played by Miles Davis.
On her "Jazz Child" CD, the rhythm section modulates to "My Funny Valentine" in measure 35.

A Being Such As You

Music and Lyric by
Walter Davis, Jr.

Big Brown Eyes

Instrumentally known as "Glo's Theme"

Music by Tommy Turrentine
Lyric by L. Aziza Miller

Sung by Meredith d'Ambrosio on Love Is For The Birds (Sunnyside SSC 1101D)

Beloved

Instrumentally known as "Daahoud"

Music by Clifford Brown
Lyric by Meredith d'Ambrosio

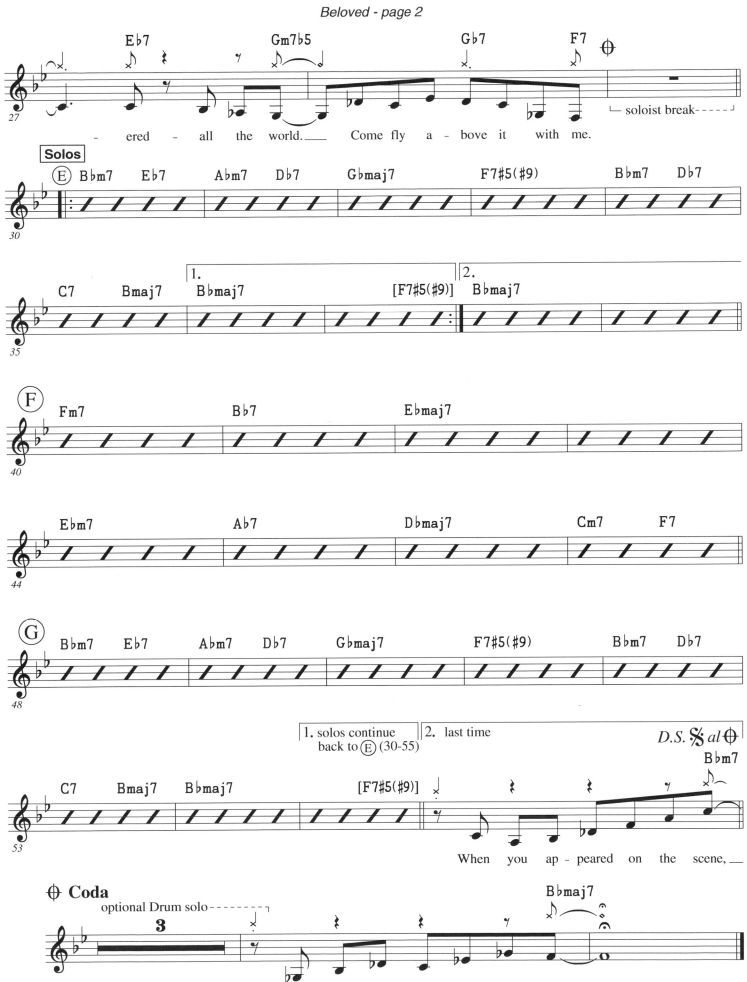

Chillin'

Instrumentally known as "Whims Of Chambers"

Music by Paul Chambers
Lyric by R. Rachel Mackin

* melody with Bass or Bass play 2-feel

Christmas Morning In The Snow

Instrumentally known as "Merry Christmas"

Music by Freddie Redd
Lyric by Van Dee Sickler

Dm

Sung by Kevin Mahogany on Songs And Moments (Enja ENJ 8072)

The Coaster

Music and Lyric by
Grachan Moncur III

Sung by Meredith d'Ambrosio on *Love Is For The Birds* (Sunnyside SSC 1101D)

Cup Of Life

Instrumentally known as "Cup Bearers"

Music by Tom McIntosh
Lyric by Meredith d'Ambrosio

Do It Again

Instrumentally known as "Mr. A.T. Revisited"

Medium swing

Music by Walter Bolden
Lyric by R. Rachel Mackin

Sung by Meredith d'Ambrosio on Love Is For The Birds (Sunnyside SSC 1101D)

Don't Go

Instrumentally known as "Josephine"

Music by Ralph Moore
Lyric by Meredith d'Ambrosio

* downstem notes are instrumental

Copyright © 1988, 1999 SECOND FLOOR MUSIC

Empty Room

Instrumentally known as "Sound Within An Empty Room"

Music by Fritz Pauer
Lyric by Mark Murphy

Sung by Chet Baker on Round Midnight original motion picture soundtrack (Columbia CK 40464 [Sony Legacy 85811])

Fair Weather

Music and Lyric by
Kenny Dorham

Sung by Kevin Mahogany on You Got What It Takes / Kevin Mahogany (Enja ENJ 9039)
Sung by ICU (Miles Griffith and Roger Holland) on Truth, Justice & The Blues / James Williams & ICU (Evidence ECD 22142)

For Old Times' Sake

Instrumentally known as "Old Times' Sake"

Music by James Williams
Lyric by Pamela Baskin-Watson

Full Moonlight

Instrumentally known as "Full Moonlight And Stars Made Of Silver"

Music by Cecil Payne
Lyric by Rob Bargad

Full moon-light, stars made of sil - ver___ shine so bright.
moon a - glow ig - nites in your eyes___ a fire - works show,

Hold-ing each oth - er___ tight, in love on a sum - mer
mak-ing my heart jump ___ so, it's love like I've nev - er

1. night. ___ The
2. known. ___

Are you a dream? A con - jured scene?

If I'm in - sane, I guess I have the moon to blame. When

heav - en cries tears made of sil - ver, the star - lit skies

make it a mag - ic ___ night, and there's no fin - er

sight than you in the full moon - light. ___

to solos
(1-28)

Garden In The Sand

Instrumentally known as "Bossa De Luxe"

Music by Hank Mobley
Lyric by Bebe Herring

The Gift Of Love

Music and Lyric by
Rodgers Grant

Heavenly!

Instrumentally known as "Tryst"

Music by Jonny King
Lyric by R. Rachel Mackin

Sung by Oscar Brown, Jr. on Then and Now (Weasel Disc 33342)

Honeydo

Music and Lyric by
Oscar Brown, Jr.

Sung by Lenora Helm and Eric Walker on People Music / Donald Brown (Muse MCD 5406)

I Love It When You Dance That Way

Music by Donald Brown
Lyric by Donald and Dorothy Brown

Em

Sung by Jeri Brown on Image In The Mirror: The Triptych (Justin Time JUST 151)

I'll Remember Love

Instrumentally known as "The Setting Sun"

Music by Milton Sealey
Lyric by Catherine Whitney

* The Bass line in the introduction continues and is prominent; it modulates with the
  pick-up to measure 13.

I'm Movin' On

Music by Kirk Nurock
Lyric by Judy Niemack

Dm

In The Moment

Instrumentally known as "For The Moment"

Music by Renee Rosnes
Lyric by Shelley Brown

Sung by Meredith d'Ambrosio on Love Is For The Birds (Sunnyside SSC 1101D)

Just A Dream

Instrumentally known as "Falando De Orlando"

Music by Eddie Higgins
Lyric by Meredith d'Ambrosio

Gm

Sung by Fleurine on Meant To Be! (Universal [Netherlands] 159 085)

It's All In The Mind

Instrumentally known as "Rejuvenate"

Music by Bobby Porcelli
Lyric by Fleurine

Just A Little Dreamer

Instrumentally known as "Chips"

Music by Elmo Hope
Lyric by R. Rachel Mackin

Medium slow swing

Sung by Vanessa Rubin on Pastiche (BMG Novus NOV 63152)

Life's Mosaic

Instrumentally known as "Mosaic"

Music by Cedar Walton
Lyric by John and Paula Hackett

Dm

Sung by Vanessa Rubin on Mean What You Say / Cecil Bridgewater (Brownstone BRCD 9802)

Like An Old Song

Instrumentally known as "Fairytale Countryside"

Music by Fritz Pauer
Lyric by Fritz Pauer and Vanessa Rubin

Eb

Sung by Abbey Lincoln on Abbey Is Blue (Riverside RLP 1153 [OJCCD 069])

Long As You're Living

Instrumentally known as "As Long As You're Living"

Music by Julian Priester &
Tommy Turrentine
Lyric by Oscar Brown, Jr.

* see discussion of blues on page 146

c

Sung by Sergio Mihanovich on B.A. Jazz (Vik 1080)
Sung by Leny Andrade on Leny Andrade (Pointer 203 0008)

Love And Deception

Music and Lyric by
Sergio Mihanovich

* pick-up to melody (A) only

Bb

Love Is Forever

Instrumentally known as "Al's Mist"

Music by Al Grey
Lyric by Meredith d'Ambrosio

Am

Sung by Betty Carter on It's Not About The Melody (Verve 314 513 870)

The Love We Had Yesterday

Music and Lyric by
Pamela Baskin-Watson

Sung by Abbey Lincoln on People In Me (Verve 314 513 626)

The Man With The Magic

Instrumentally known as "Dorian"

Music by Ronnie Mathews
Lyric by Abbey Lincoln

Ab

Sung by Fleurine on Meant To Be! (Universal [Netherlands] 159 085)

Meant To Be!

Instrumentally known as "Chicken An' Dumplins"

Music by Ray Bryant
Lyric by Fleurine

Medium swing

Intro

melody

Ev-'ry

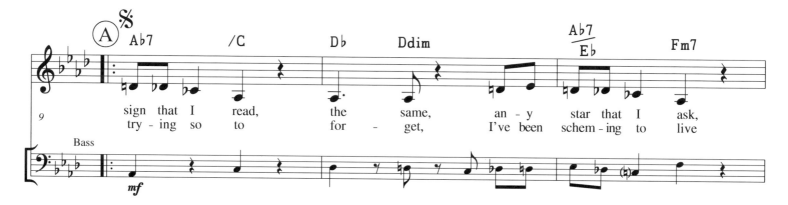

sign that I read, the same, an-y star that I ask,
try-ing so to for - get, I've been schem-ing to live

no ta-boo, ev-'ry move that I make, in - sane, ev-'ry
diff - 'rent-ly, and al - though it's a - gainst all odds all the

road that I take leads to you. I've been you and me.
witch - es re - peat,

* pick-up to melody Ⓐ only

Fm

Sung by Lambert, Hendricks and Ross on The Hottest New Group In Jazz (Columbia CL 1403 [Sony C2K 64933])

Moanin'

Medium swing

Music by Bobby Timmons
Lyric by Jon Hendricks

* melody Ⓐ and Ⓒ sections are "call and response" style: vocal break followed by instrumental or vocal response.

Eb

Sung by Ben Sidran on Bop City (Antilles AN 1012)
Sung by Kevin Mahogany on You Got What It Takes (Enja ENJ 9039)

My Little Sherri

Instrumentally known as "Little Sherri"

Music by Charlie Rouse
Lyric by Ben Sidran

* or solo chorus could be 1-12

Bb

Sung by Karin Krog on If You Could See Me Now / Per Husby (Gemini GMCD89)

Never Been In Love

Walking ballad

Music by Tadd Dameron
Lyric by Irving Reid

Bb

Sung by Eddie Jefferson on Body And Soul (Prestige PR 7619 [OJCCD 396])
Sung by Kevin Mahogany on Kevin Mahogany (Warner Bros 46226)

Oh! Gee!

Medium up swing

Music and Lyric by
Matthew Gee

* see discussion of the blues on page 146

Gm

Sung by Tina May on One Fine Day (33 Records 33JAZZ 050)

One Fine Day

Instrumentally known as "Cubano Chant"

Music by Ray Bryant
Lyric by L. Aziza Miller

Your smile is my joy and laugh - ter, you're the one I knew my heart was af - ter. My feel - ings were an in - di - go blue un - til one fine day I met ____ you. The look in your eyes so ten - der, ev - 'ry kiss, a si - lent wish re - mem - bered. Nev - er had ____ a clue ____ my lone - ly days were all through un - til one fine day I met ____ you. You've giv - en me a new rea - son to sing. Gone a - way ____ the tears, I

Sung by Kurt Elling on Flirting With Twilight (Blue Note 31113)

Orange Blossoms In Summertime

Instrumentally known as "Orange Blossom"

Music by Curtis Lundy
Lyric by Kurt Elling

B♭m

Medium slow swing

One Heart's Dream

Instrumentally known as "Now That The Pain Is Gone"

Music by Rodgers Grant
Lyric by Catherine Whitney

Our Love Remains

Instrumentally known as "Love Remains"

Music by Robert Watson and Pamela Baskin-Watson
Lyric by Pamela Baskin-Watson

Sung by Meredith d'Ambrosio on Love Is For The Birds (Sunnyside SSC 1101D)

Rhyme Of Spring

Instrumentally known as "Poetic Spring"

Music by Kenny Dorham
Lyric by Meredith d'Ambrosio

Sea Breeze

Samba

Music and Lyric by
Jon Burr

E♭m

Sung by Eddie Jefferson on Letter From Home (Riverside RLP 9411 [OJCCD 307])

Soft And Furry

Music by Johnny Griffin
Lyric by Eddie Jefferson

* pick-up to melody Ⓐ only

A Something In A Summer's Day

Music by Kirk Nurock
Lyric adapted from a poem
by Emily Dickinson*

* XII: Psalm Of The Day (Nature)

Sung by Dinah Washington on The Complete Dinah Washington on Mercury, vol. 3 (Mercury 834 675)
Also used in The Bridges Of Madison County motion picture soundtrack (Malpaso 45949)

Soft Winds

Music by Fletcher Henderson
Lyric by Fred Royal

Sung by Irene Kral on Kral Space (Catalyst 7625 [Collectables COL-CD 7160])

Sometime Ago

Music and Lyric by
Sergio Mihanovich

Slowly with expression (ballad)

B♭m

Sung by Abbey Lincoln on Straight Ahead (Candid CM 8015 [Candid 79015])
Sung by Jeannie Lee on After Hours / Jeanne Lee-Mal Waldron (Owl 077 830993)

Straight Ahead

Music by Mal Waldron
Lyric by Abbey Lincoln

F

Sung by Gloria Cooper on Day By Day (GAC Music GAC 1001)

Sweet And True

Instrumentally known as "Sweetness"

Music by Curtis Fuller
Lyric by Catherine Whitney

Medium swing

G

Sung by Meredith d'Ambrosio on Love Is For The Birds (Sunnyside SSC 1101D)

That Magic Rapture

Instrumentally known as "Rapture"

Music by Harold Land
Lyric by Meredith d'Ambrosio

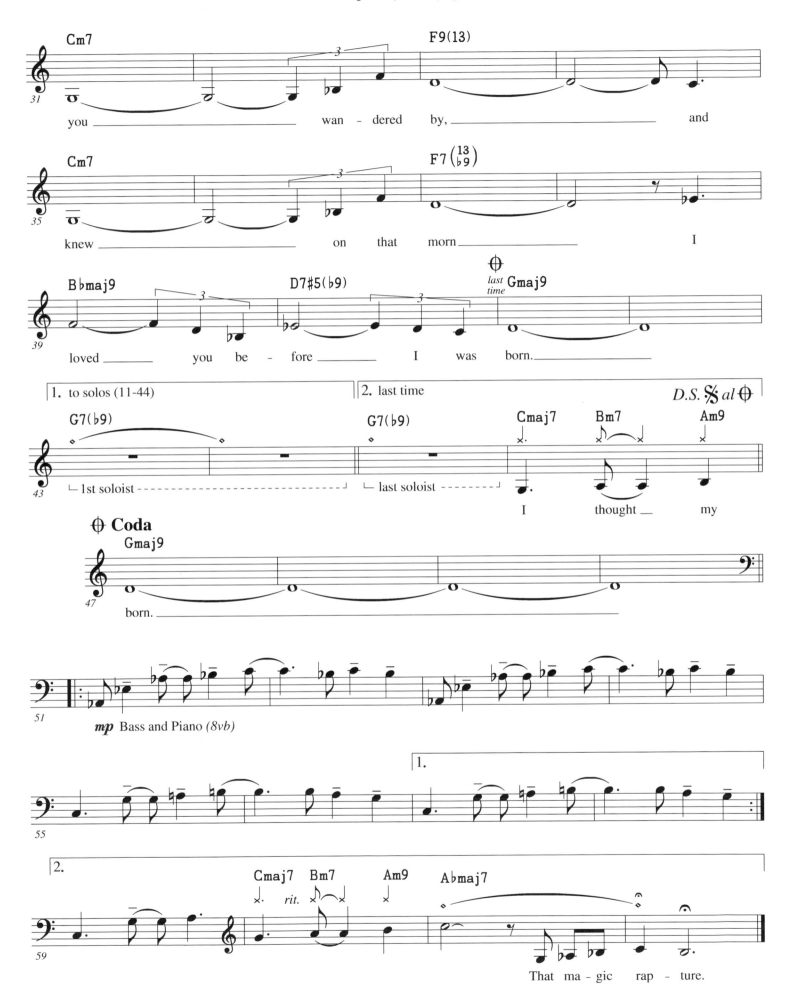

Sung by Georgie Fame on If You Could See Me Now / Per Husby (Gemini GMCD 89)

There's No More Blue Time

Instrumentally known as "A Blue Time"

Music by Tadd Dameron
Lyric by Georgie Fame

Medium slow swing

In no con-di-tion ____ to play my part ev-er since you
ac-tion ____ a-round the scene, try-ing to for-
last chorus: I've turned the cor-ner, ____ I'm go-ing straight, got you in my

left and broke my heart. My po-si-tion is de-
get what might have been. Sat-is-fac-tion nev-er
sights and just can't wait. Oh, my dear, ____ we won't spend

cid-ed-ly un-sure, and now I find I can't cope an-y
seems to come my way, a-las, and now I go from day to
an-y time a-part since you some-how have soothed my ach-ing

more. I'm head-ing for a real blue time 'cause I can't get you
day try'n' hard to lose these time-less blues. I'm re-signed to a
heart. I've said good-bye to my blue time, I'm real gone and I

1.
out of my mind. Look-ing for ver-y blue time.

2.   *to solos (1-12)*
                                          after solos
                                          to last chorus (D.C. al ⊕)

⊕ **Coda**

hope you don't mind 'cause I know from now on ev-'ry-

thing will be fine. There's no more blue time. ____

Copyright © 1961 (renewed 1989), 1995 TWENTY-EIGHTH STREET MUSIC

Eb

Sung by Annie Ross on King Pleasure and Annie Ross Sing (Prestige 7128 [OJC 217])

Twisted

Music by Wardell Gray
Lyric by Annie Ross

Medium swing

* To solos (Blues) or continue on with the pick-up to Annie Ross' lyric to Wardell Gray's
  three Tenor Sax solo choruses (next 2 pages). If this vocal solo is not performed, sing the
  pick-up to Ⓐ in the last measure of the last solo chorus (see m.58) into lyric 1, then 3 to **Coda**.

Tomorrow

Music and Lyric by
Lonnie Hillyer

Two Reflect As One

Instrumentally known as "Waltz No. 1"

Music by Michael Cochrane
Lyric by Cheryl Pyle

Medium swing

A Bm7b5   E7#5(#9)   Am9   Ab9(13)

Fig - ures
shad - ows

yearn - ing,
ghost - ly

Gm9   Gb7#5(#9)   Fmaj9   B7($^{13}_{b9}$)

spin   like   fall   leaves   turn - ing.
touch   the   full   moon   close - ly,

Qui - et - ly
ex - pres - sions

Bm7b5/E   Bb9(13)   Am9   Gb7#5(#9)

danc - ing
glis - ten

du - o,
un - der

1.

F9sus   E7($^{#11}_{b9}$)   Am

shad - ed eve - ning glow,   in   the   branch - like

2.

F9sus   E7($^{#11}_{b9}$)   Dm/A   Am

sky _____ lit in - di - go.

B Ab9(#11)   G9sus   Gb7(#9)   F9sus

Cir - cling pat - terns, grace - ful

Dm/E   Ebmaj9   D9sus   Db7#5(#9)

steps   so   old   yet   new,

B♭

Sung by Dave Frishberg on Let's Eat Home (Concord CCD 4402)

The Underdog

Music by Al Cohn
Lyric by Dave Frishberg

Medium slow swing

(A) Gm · Fm6 · E♭maj7 · D7

Here I go a-gain, __ a-bout to drop an-oth-er bun-dle on the

D♭9♭5 · C7(♭9) · E♭m7 · A♭7 · Dm9 · D♭9(6)

un-der-dog, the un-der-dog. __ Is-n't it a shame, but

G♭maj7 · F7(♯9) · B♭m7 · B♭7(♯9) · E♭7 · D7(♭9)

that's the kind of game I play.

(B) Gm · D/F♯ · Fm6 · B♭9

Peo-ple think it's fun-ny if they see you've got your mon-ey on the

E♭maj9 · E♭6 · Em9 · A7♯5 · Fm7 · B♭7

clown. When the chips are down, and when your side gets out-

Dm7 · G9 · E♭m7 · A♭9 · Cm9 · F7

classed they say, "Nice guys wind up last." But there's a

(C) B♭ · E7♯5 · E♭maj7 · D7

strange sat-is-fac-tion, when you're put-ting all your ac-tion on the

C

Sung by Jean Turner on Some Women I've Known / Stan Kenton (Creative World ST 1029)

Warm Blue Stream

Music by Sara Cassey
Lyric by Dotty Wayne

Sung by Gloria Lynne on After Hours (Everest SDBR 1063 [Collectables COL 5853])

F

We Never Kissed
(What A Shame)

Music and Lyric by
Melba Liston

B♭

Sung by Daryl Sherman on I Hear Music / Ruby Braff (Arbors ARCD 19244)

We're All Through

Music and Lyric by
Ruby Braff

Sung by the Manhattan Vocal Project on When We Meet Again

When We Meet Again

Instrumentally known as "Utopia"

Music by Scott Whitfield
Lyric by Michael Andrew

Sung by Tuck & Patti on Paradise Found / Tuck & Patti (Windham Hill 11336)

When We're Alone

Instrumentally known as "Joy Spring"

Music by Clifford Brown
Lyric by Michael Stillman

Sung by Jeri Brown on Image In The Mirror: The Triptych (Justin Time JUST 151)

Who's Been Loving You?

Instrumentally known as "Blue Love"

Music by Milton Sealey
Lyric by L. Aziza Miller

B♭

Sung by Meredith d'Ambrosio on Echo Of A Kiss (Sunnyside SSC 1078D)

Why Do I Still Dream Of You?

Music and Lyric by
Meredith d'Ambrosio

Bb

Sung by Meredith d'Ambrosio on Echo Of A Kiss (Sunnyside SSC 1078D)

Without Reason, Without Rhyme

Music and Lyric by
Meredith d'Ambrosio

Without You

Instrumentally known as "Malaga Moon"

Music by Renee Rosnes
Lyric by Shelley Brown

You Are Mine
(A Lullaby Of Motherhood)

Music and Lyric by
Norman Simmons

Sung by Ernestine Anderson on Nica's Tempo / Gigi Gryce (Savoy MG 12137)

You'll Always Be The One I Love

Music and Lyric by
Gigi Gryce

Sung by Gloria Cooper on Day By Day (GAC Music GAC 1001)

You Know Who!

Music and Lyric by
Bertha Hope

Sung by Jimmy Scott on Everybody's Somebody's Fool (Coral 60825 [GRP 669])

You Never Miss The Water
Till The Well Runs Dry

Music and Lyric by
Lucky Thompson

Slow bluesy swing

Sung by ICU (Miles Griffith and Roger Holland) on Truth, Justice & The Blues / James Williams (Evidence ECD 22142)
Sung by Mark Murphy on Some Time Ago (High Note HCD 7048)

You're My Alter Ego

Instrumentally known as "Alter Ego"

Music by James Williams
Lyric by Pamela Baskin-Watson

THE LYRICS ALONE

ALL MY LOVE, ESPECIALLY FOR YOU
music by John Oddo, lyric by Pamela Baskin-Watson

Lying here all by myself
as the dawn turns into day,
I'm wond'ring if you're all by yourself
wondering the same of me.
Thinking of the days we've spent
and all the nights that drifted by,
I begin to see just how good we are together, you and I.

You became a friend to me
just when I thought my friends were few.
I never thought I could love someone
half as much as I love you.
Just when I began to feel
that I was ready to give my heart,
those doubts and fears that I tried to hide
began to tear us apart.

Now that I've had the time
to think of all we've shared together,
I know I'll never find another love so good.
So lover, if you'll please forgive
the way I turned and ran away,
I'm ready now if you want to take a chance on me again,
my friend, and all of my love will be especially for you.

coda
All my love will be especially for you.

ALONE AGAIN
music and lyric by J.R. Monterose

Here I am alone again
and now I feel I understand
just who I am, what I am,
why I am, just realizing
I must be free of ev'rything
that could possibly inhibit me
from doing what I have to do.

Here I am alone again
but now I have the strength to reveal
just what I would want to be
and nothing else could make me feel
that I should ever bow my head in shame
for how I feel, so here I am alone again.

ALONE WITH JUST MY DREAMS
music and lyric by George Duvivier

Alone with just my dreams
all else is gone,
nothing left it seems,
just memories and haunting melodies remain.

Alone with just my dreams,
tears cloud the moon,
gone are all its beams.
When stars appear
it seems they want to hear your voice once again.

Oh, why did this have to happen?
I ask myself is it true?
Is it fair that I suffer so
just for falling in love
with someone such as you?

Why try to carry on?
Life's just a shell
now that you are gone.
Does fate decree that I must always be
alone with just my dreams?

ANOTHER TIME, ANOTHER PLACE
music by Robert Watson, lyric by Pamela Baskin-Watson

[whispered]   Make . . . time . . . stand . . . still . . .
(I want to) Make . . . time . . . stand . . . still . . .

[sung] So much time has come and gone, it's been so long
I just can't wait to see him/her.
Ev'ry time I close my eyes, you fill my mind.
I'm just afraid I've lost him/her.

Another time, another place,
how will it feel?

We let life get in the way;
will life our love betray
or will it make our hearts grow fonder?
Many diff'rent points of view between me and you;
is this more than I should hope for?

Another time, another space.
Will it be real?

I let him/her go.
I've got to know if there's a chance
that I can still be with him/her.

coda (vamp)
[whispered]   Make . . . time . . . stand . . . still . . .

ANOTHER WORLD
music and lyric by Rob Bargad

I dreamed of a love I'll never know,
of a place I'll never go, another world.

I woke so in love that it hurts me so
and now I need to go
to that other world.

The pain that fills me now
will never, ever end,
the love I feel,
it isn't real, it's just pretend.
If only I could sleep and dream on endlessly,
I'd leave this world
and hope that world comes back to me.

I'm lost in a strange and lonely love
for we will only love in another world.

BABY, I'M COMING HOME
music and lyric by Chuck Wayne

I thought that I was oh, so smart
and that I could make it alone,
but now I know I can't fool my heart
so baby, I'm coming home.

I guess I just sorta missed my cue
the day I decided to roam,
and now I know there's no one but you
so baby, I'm coming home.

I'll tie a string around my finger
to remind me of that fateful day.
If you'll be kind, forgive and forget,
never again will I stray so.

It doesn't matter what the future may bring,
for all of my past I'll atone.
Call up the preacher,
I've got the ring
and baby, I'm coming home.

BALLAD FOR MILES
music and lyric by Sheila Jordan

When Miles Davis played a ballad,
what could be more beautiful than hearing Miles
at the Village Vanguard in the nineteen sixties
with Paul Chambers, Wynton Kelly,
Jimmy Cobb and John, John Coltrane.
I heard Miles play a song
and in my heart I sang along.
When Miles Davis played a ballad,
what could be more beautiful than hearing Miles, Miles.

A BEING SUCH AS YOU
music and lyric by Walter Davis, Jr.

The face you wear, I've seen it before,
can't you tell by the look I give you?
I won't say it was in a dream,
tho' dreams aren't always what they seem.

The way you smile just turns me right on.
Seems so familiar, I'm paranoid.
Won't you give me just one clue?
I'm going crazy over you.

It might have been in another world
when my love was unfurled to you.
There's something tellin' me it's true.

I want to know you better each day
before the heavens take you away.
I feel a change that's strange and new,
to love a being such as you.

BELOVED

music by Clifford Brown, lyric by Meredith d'Ambrosio

When you appeared on the scene,
suddenly I didn't know what to say,
for the way that you smiled at me
nearly blew me away!

Oh, baby, where have you been?
I don't wanna love you just for a day,
or for even a while, you see,
'cause I'm planning to stay.

Give me one little kiss.
Show me you're mine, all mine.
I've been waiting for this.
Send me a sign. It'll be fine.

So, tell me what'll it be?
Can't you see that we will never be blue?
I will always belong to you,
my beloved. It's true.

It's time, my beloved,
you discovered all the world.
Come fly above it with me.

coda
It's time, beloved, to fly.

Copyright © 1962 (renewed 1990), 2000 Second Floor Music

BIG BROWN EYES

music by Tommy Turrentine, lyric by L. Aziza Miller

Big brown eyes,
let me know,
should I stay or should I go?

Hey, big brown eyes,
tell me, please,
are you playing games with me?

Nature's prize,
mere words cannot explain
the joy I feel
each time you call my name, oh!

You're the page
in my book,
big brown eyes, yes, I am hooked.

It's no secret,
let the record show
the word is out and ev'rybody knows it.

Look closely
and you'll see
love's inside these big brown eyes.

Copyright © 1991, 1996 Second Floor Music

CHILLIN'

music by Paul Chambers, lyric by R. Rachel Mackin

[1] Most of my friends go to the club Friday night,
standin' on line, tryin' to find Mister Right/a Ms. Right.
But now I am off the scene,
I found my dream,
the deluxe sundae with the cherry and cream.
My future's lookin' very bright,
I'm chillin' with my baby tonight,
chillin' tonight.

[2] My friends, just listen up and please, be polite,
because I'm chillin' with my baby tonight.
You better not ring that phone,
don't lean on the bell,
'cause we'll be here and things'll start in to jell.
Survey the site by satellite,
I'm chillin' with my baby tonight,
chillin' tonight.

[3] It will be five hundred degrees Fahrenheit
when I am chillin' with my baby tonight.
Now anything more than two
would be a crowd,
so what I'm sayin', let us stay in our cloud.
Don't ruin our height while we're in flight,
I'm chillin' with my baby tonight,
chillin' tonight.

[4] In a big rush to straighten up,
make things right,
for when I'm chillin' with my baby tonight.
Oh, I gotta slow it down,
and try to be calm,
can't wait to see him/her,
lead him/her to my salon.
Oh, I am so excited 'cause
I'm chillin' with my baby tonight,
chillin' tonight,
baby, tonight!

Copyright © 1956 (renewed 1984), 1996 Second Floor Music
and Twenty-Eighth Street Music

CHRISTMAS MORNING IN THE SNOW
music by Freddie Redd, lyric by Van Dee Sickler

Deep, the snows of late December,
white, the nights of crystal splendor.
These are things that we remember,
walking in the snow together.
While the snowflakes in the lamplight
shine like diamonds in your hair,
we feel in the gentle hush of twilight,
heaven's promise, that by daylight,
we'll have Christmas (Merry Christmas).

Wake me gently in the morning,
just as Christmas day is dawning.
Let me be the first to whisper;
"Merry Christmas, Merry Christmas!"
Let's get dressed and go out strolling,
out walking in the snow.
We'll find in the circle of the lamplight,
there'll be snowdrifts on our doorstep,
and it's Christmas, (Merry Christmas) Merry Christmas.

THE COASTER
music and lyric by Grachan Moncur III

Grooving high,
coasting over the waves of the sea,
all the stars up above do smile.

Gliding fire
sparkles from the flare in your hand,
riding high on your dream of love.

Come with me
in my arms
to a world
full of charms.

Come with me
in my arms
to a world
of all charms.

Grooving high,
coasting over the waves of the sea,
all the stars up above do smile.

coda (vamp)
up above do smile,
up above do smile.

CUP OF LIFE
music by Tom McIntosh, lyric by Meredith d'Ambrosio

Deep inside lives a dream I hide.
It's a message sent from up above
meant for the one I love.
If you would say to me,
"Come run away with me!"
you will see
we will be cup bearers,
you and me.

Drink it slow.
Feel the glow.
Love's the water of life;
it's the one thing that all the world should know.

Hear my song,
and before too long
it will set us free
if you will sip
my cup of life with me.
No need to wonder how.
Just seize the moment now.
Set your goal.
Let it flow
into your heart and soul.

DO IT AGAIN
music by Walter Bolden, lyric by R. Rachel Mackin

Oh, do it again.
Do that thing you do with your eyes,
the one that makes my temp'rature rise
when you gaze those baby blue eyes, they hypnotize me.

Do it again.
Do that thing you do with your smile,
the one that makes my heart do the mile.
I have lost my veteran style, I'm a juvenile!

Bang, bang, hit me again,
clang, clang, I can't recall when
I ever felt this before.
Oh, please now, do it some more.

Oh, do it again.
Say some words that I'll never hear
because I'm fantasizing, my dear,
how I'm wanting you to be near.
Come on over here.

DON'T GO

music by Ralph Moore, lyric by Meredith d'Ambrosio

Don't go. Linger awhile.
Stay with me all through the night.
Come close. Show me a smile.
We're all alone, out of sight.

Whisper to me little things in my ear.
Tell me the time is here for deep passion.
Touch me. No one will know.
Now there's a fire. Make it grow.

Kiss me. Fill my desire.
Love will belong to us soon,
here in the glow of the moon.

Copyright © 1988, 1999 Second Floor Music

EMPTY ROOM

music by Fritz Pauer, lyric by Mark Murphy

The sound within an empty room,
asleep or waking,
day or at night,
as I push this stupid broom
around this echoing room
to sweep away all the gloom.

Those mem'ries of that silly night,
the quarrels haunt my dreams,
"Never-Never Land" time
taking me somewhere alone with you,
just you and your fancies fooling me.

You Gods! Can you tell me
what is true or false now, please now?
Do I stay? Do I go now?
Do I make the first move or does he/she?

The stories go on endlessly,
can I clear out the pain?
Maybe music and fun,
invited here for just a moment or two,
might be the way that I could quiet all this noise.

Those taunting sounds of you and the past!
It's really the time
this empty room says.
All empty rooms
are waiting for new sound,
the friendly sounds of love.

last time
and laughter soon!

Copyright © 1984, 1999 Second Floor Music and Twenty-Eighth Street Music

FAIR WEATHER

music and lyric by Kenny Dorham

When we walk side by side, like brothers,
ol' glory will stand up and whirl,
the trumpet will blow
as it never has blown before.
There'd be fair weather together,

side by side, it would never end.
Hate would die, love would win.
Go forth, hero.

Peace on earth
and good will to all
who make it divine and so real.
Plant seeds of kind deeds
like the trees
and of course love will grow.

Money doesn't fit into this scheme of things,
how can a house be built on angel wings?
Fair weather, together,
fair weather, my friend.

Copyright © 1959 (renewed 1987) Second Floor Music

FOR OLD TIMES' SAKE

music by James Williams, lyric by Pamela Baskin-Watson

Old friends, old foes, old photographs,
old places we would go for laughs,
all the things we shared as lovers' fun
we still can share as old friends,
except for one!

Old anecdotes, old tired jokes, old TV shows,
and oh, isn't it wonderful
that such good friends we make,
and we can smile for old times' sake.

Copyright © 1985, 1986 Second Floor Music

FULL MOONLIGHT
music by Cecil Payne, lyric by Rob Bargad

Full moonlight,
stars made of silver
shine so bright.
Holding each other tight,
in love on a summer night.

The moon aglow
ignites in your eyes
a fireworks show,
making my heart jump so,
it's love like I've never known.

Are you a dream?
A conjured scene?
If I'm insane,
I guess I have the moon to blame.

When heaven cries
tears made of silver,
the starlit skies
make it a magic night,
and there's no finer sight
than you in the full moonlight.

GARDEN IN THE SAND
music by Hank Mobley, lyric by Bebe Herring

This garden grows in the sand,
without the benefit of rain,
the flowers red and vain
under Saharan sun.

This garden glows in my hands,
with emerald and sapphire light,
all amethyst at night
under Saharan stars.

The sand, just like the sea, is whisp'ring to me:
"These flowers are too fragile and frail to be . . . ."

My garden knows, understands,
that even in this hostile land,
what grows will somehow thrive:
on love it will survive.

Beyond my tall garden wall,
a coverlet of snow in June,
a nightingale at noon:
the world all upside down.

But in this garden I sleep,
and fountains play my lullabies,
away from unseen eyes,
this world my very own.

The desert keeps a secret these walls conceal:
a kingdom that's too perfect to be revealed.

My garden grows, out of time,
forever in this hostile clime,
and it will somehow thrive:
on love it will survive.

THE GIFT OF LOVE
music and lyric by Rodgers Grant

You welcomed love from someone you hold dear,
there are little doubts and even fears.
Just think of this gift you've been given.
He/she speaks to you tenderly,
open up your mind and you'll see
his/her eyes, spark'ling in the sun,
telling you you're the only one.

Then he'll/she'll smile, giving from his/her soul unselfishly
unrequited love, so pure and free,
free as a leaf gently falling.
Apprehensions take their leave,
you will know the truth and believe.
Your mind, it will open wide
and your love, it will find a way to his/her heart.

HEAVENLY!

music by Jonny King, lyric by R. Rachel Mackin

Once in a while
to bring on a smile
the stars get together
and chart out a plan,
and one magical night,
for fun and delight,
they sent me to you,
you to me,
heavenly!

I never knew
an angel like you,
an angel who moves me
the way that you do,
and I thank all the stars
for their gift from afar
sending me to you,
you to me,
heavenly!

HONEYDO

music and lyric by Oscar Brown, Jr.

By the job I hold down
I'm put sorely to the test,
so when it comes quittin' time
I surely do need rest.
But at home I can't relax
due to "honeydo" attacks:
"Honey do this, honey do that,
honey do the other."
Oh, brother.

Time I finish with one task
my wife dreams up two more,
there's no favor she won't ask,
no errand and no chore.
Even though I do resist
she has her ways to insist:
"Honey do this, honey do that,
honey do the other."

Some further duty to be done,
another load that weighs a ton,
because I was the mother's son
caught in that lover's web she spun.
Now 'fore the day is scarce begun,
well past the setting of the sun,
the woman has me on the run.
I want some fun, get next to none.

If you've made the marriage scene
you ought to understand.
Husbands are a cross between
a hero and a hand
hired to help around the house,
doing odd jobs for his spouse.
"Honey do this, honey do that,
honey do the other."
Oh, brother.

coda
"Honey do this, honey do that,
honey do this, honey do that,
honey do this, honey do that,
honey do the other."
Oh, brother! Then,
"Honey do this, honey do that,
honey do this, honey do that,
honey do this, honey do that,
honey do the other."
Oh, brother!

I LOVE IT WHEN YOU DANCE THAT WAY
music by Donald Brown, lyric by Donald and Dorothy Brown

Right now I just have to say,
I love it when you dance that way.
You're the best thing that I've seen today
and it feels very good to be near you
to dance the night away.
I want to feel you, touch you.

I know that I shouldn't say
it's sexy when you dance that way.
You're the reason that I'm here today
and I hope you'll give me a chance just to dance with you,
I'm in love with you.

Closer, will you dance my way,
inviting me to stay the day?
I'm so glad that you are here today
and the night air feels warmer around you,
let's dance the night away.
I want to hold you, love you.

You know, I've just got to say,
it's sexy when you dance that way.
Love is moving in on me today.
Take my heart and my body away
and I'll dance with you,
so in love with you.

Copyright © 1990 Second Floor Music

I'LL REMEMBER LOVE
music by Milton Sealey, lyric by Catherine Whitney

I forgot the words that you said to me,
    (I remember now)
it was true that I couldn't see your point of view.
    (I remember now)
The words you spoke so easily seemed
too cold to be
our destiny,
so now our love stops,
we wonder why.
    (I remember now, I remember now)

Could a love like ours ever end this way,
    (can't our love be strong?)
did our hearts reveal honest love, how could it be?
    (can't our love be strong?).
For thoughts of all those nights by the fire,
and now you're gone,
I was so wrong
for turning my back,
and now love dies.
    (can't our love be strong, could our love be wrong?)

The sadness of a love gone away is pain.
    (you'll remember too)
It used to be so easy to laugh but now there're tears.
    (you'll remember too)
No matter how much time one can pray
for better days
to find new love,
our hearts must now stop,
we'll love again.
    (I'll remember then, I'll remember then)

Who could think that lovers could turn to friends?
    (I'll remember love)
Those memories of all that was good will never end,
    (I'll remember love)
and painful thoughts of separate hearts
that could not see
reality,
but love that was lost
will always be.
    (I'll remember love, I'll remember love)
vamp
    (I'll remember love, I'll remember love)

Copyright © 1990, 1997 Second Floor Music and Twenty-Eighth Street Music

I'M MOVIN' ON
music by Kirk Nurock, lyric by Judy Niemack

I've been collecting things,
too many people attaching strings,
I've got to spread my wings
'cause I'm movin' on.

I'm tired of looking back.
Hindsight reveals only what I lack.
History fades to black
'cause I'm movin' on.

How can I just let go
when mem'ries pull my spirit so.?
I'd like to fly away, start again.

Wind on a desert night,
blow past a million stars sparkling bright,
lift me and guide my flight
'cause I'm movin' on.

coda
Movin' on!

Copyright © 1997 Second Floor Music

IN THE MOMENT
music by Renee Rosnes, lyric by Shelley Brown

Footprints in the sand,
ashes by a hearth,
fallen leaves that land
on a path.

Pebbles in a stream,
shadows on the ground,
all is like a dream standing still

and in the moment
I look around me
and all I see is time suspended.

Songs that once were sung,
laughter now is gone,
bells that once were rung,
quiet now.

Copyright © 1990, 2000 Second Floor Music

IT'S ALL IN THE MIND
music by Bobby Porcelli, lyric by Fleurine

Rejuvenate,
get old thoughts out of your mind,
let a fresh wind blow and soon you'll see,
the things you have been fearing,
those circles in your brain searing,
will simply be history.

It's all in the mind,
so if you have faith
you will rejuvenate.

Rejuvenate,
open windows in your head,
let your hangups fly right out the door!

Let go now!
Make a brand new start!

Copyright © 1983, 1995 Second Floor Music

JUST A DREAM
music by Eddie Higgins, lyric by Meredith d'Ambrosio

Midnight breezes whisper through the willow.
Distant music floats across the bay.
Moonlight shadows touch my pillow.
Sorrow seems so far away.

Morning comes and fills my room with sunlight.
Were you real, or not what you might seem?
Will you not return at midnight,
leaving me with just a dream?

coda
Leaving me with just a dream?

Copyright © 1998 Second Floor Music and Twenty-Eighth Street Music

JUST A LITTLE DREAMER
music by Elmo Hope, lyric by R. Rachel Mackin

Why does my heart pit-a-pat,
does it rat-a-tat-tat
ev'ry time that I hear
the ol' phone beginning to jingle?
Why am I all a-tingle?
It's because my heart is just a dreamer.

Crazy in love with the way
that you walk and the way
that you talk ev'ry time
that you tell the sweetest of white lies,
oh, how I wish my heart would
Smarten up and realize.

It's very plain from the things you do
that you're only playing a game
but what adventure to be
a moth that is drawn to the flame of you.

Why does my heart keep
pretending that you really care
when, for love, I am sure
that it won't be a winning season?
I can tell you the reason,
it's because my heart is just a little dreamer!

LIFE'S MOSAIC
music by Cedar Walton, lyric by John and Paula Hackett

Sounds from the East
come to life in this our home.
Turn, face the sun,
feel it rise and bring the dawn.

Think about a rainbow pure,
see the many colors there.
From many worlds
all of us must live as one.

Life is a mosaic we can create each day.

Wake, night is gone,
be a part of day's new song.

Turn, face the sun,
feel it rise and bring the dawn.

Now just for a moment, say
we will come together, pray.

Born from these sounds,
all our lives become as one.

Life is a mosaic we can create each day.

LIKE AN OLD SONG
music by Fritz Pauer, lyric by Fritz Pauer and Vanessa Rubin

In my dream I've found
such a beautiful countryside.
A door just opened wide
with fairy tales inside
and many things to hide,
mem'ries of an old song.

Sounds I hear are oh,
so familiar, they seem to be
arriving from a place
that has no time or space.
So real you could embrace
voices from an old song.

Close your eyes and see
all the things that you want to be,
make them reality.
They're not beyond the stars
like Jupiter and Mars,
they're within you like an old song.

In our lives we search
outside for what lies within.
Push ev'rything aside
and come and take a ride.
The journey's deep inside,
endless, like an old song.

coda (vamp)
like an old song, like an old song.

LONG AS YOU'RE LIVING

music by Julian Priester and Tommy Turrentine, lyric by Oscar Brown, Jr.

Ⓐ *melody*

Forgive me if I seem to preach
but there is something that I want to say,
a message that I hope will reach
the people who are throwing life away.

I call it my philosophy
and that is why I pass it on to you,
because it works so well for me
and helps me get away from strife.

I hope you'll listen carefully,
they say that truth will make you free
and that's the way you want to be,
'cause brother, this is your life.

Ⓑ *melody*

[1] Long as you're living always remember
time is for spending but there's an ending.
While you are sleeping lifetime is creeping,
wake up and taste it, foolish to waste it.
Sample and savor all of its flavor,
long as you're living.

[2] Long as you're living always remember
folks who are lazy are playing crazy.
Better keep moving, keep on improving,
you won't be hurried after you're buried.
Live ev'ry minute, put yourself in it
long as you're living.

[3] Long as you're living always remember
you'll never beat life, don't try to cheat life.
All men are brothers, do unto others,
love's for enjoying, hate's for destroying.
Never forget it or you'll regret it
long as you're living.

Ⓐ *melody*

Forgive me if I seem to preach
but there was something that I had to say,
a message that I hope will reach
the people who are throwing life away.

I call it my philosophy
and that is why I pass it on to you,
because it works so well for me
and helps me get away from strife.

I hope you'll listen carefully,
they say that truth will make you free
and that's the way you want to be,
'cause brother, this is your life.

LOVE AND DECEPTION

music and lyric by Sergio Mihanovich

Love and deception
have a strange connection.
When you love somebody
and he/she doesn't love you,
moonlight and magic
turn out to be tragic,
the play goes dramatic,
the comedy's through.

Soon there's tomorrow
when you're full of sorrow
and you'd like to borrow
someone's own happiness.
Don't be too gentle
or too sentimental
for love and deception
have a connection, I guess.

LOVE IS FOREVER

music by Al Grey, lyric by Meredith d'Ambrosio

Love is forever, not for an hour;
bound like a flower to grow, 'though its

delicate petals fade in a moment
when you allow it to go.

In a while your smile will vanish
to the dark grey mist of night.

So, you must never lose sight.
Water your blossom,
bathe it with passion,
fill ev'ry dream if it's right.

THE LOVE WE HAD YESTERDAY

music and lyric by Pamela Baskin-Watson

Suddenly time went by
leaving me here left to cry, I can't believe
the love we had yesterday has gone away!

All of the dreams we shared,
kisses that left me feeling so real,
are mem'ries now stored away.

Maybe we felt something was wrong
but we ignored it, hoping that it would pass.
Time left its mark and pulled us apart
with all those words that we didn't say,
moments we didn't get to share.

Things that were once once so real,
visions we both used to see, are now a dream
that slowly faded away.

last time
that dream of love yesterday.

THE MAN WITH THE MAGIC

music by Ronnie Mathews, lyric by Abbey Lincoln

The man who has the magic
just waves his wand and weaves a spell.
The man who has the magic
must know a secret he won't tell.

He's a high lord and master,
ooh! mischievous scamp.
Did he discover
old man Aladdin's lamp?

His eyes are like the sunrise,
he's lightning fast and fancy free
'cause he knows some razzle-dazzle.
He's got his mind on sorcery.

He's a high lord and master,
ooh! mischievous scamp.
Did he discover
old man Aladdin's lamp?

The man who has the magic
has got a way that is divine
and magically the magic is,
the magic man is mine.

MEANT TO BE!

music by Ray Bryant, lyric by Fleurine

Ev'ry sign that I read, the same,
any star that I ask, no taboo,
ev'ry move that I make, insane,
ev'ry road that I take leads to you.

I've been trying so to forget,
I've been scheming to live diff'rently,
and although it's against all odds
all the witches repeat, you and me.

It's crystal clear, it's plain to see,
they all announce we're meant to be,
obviously.
It's impossible to ignore
what the wind whispers into my ear,
all the birds sing the same song too,
only you, my love, you fail to hear.

MOANIN'
music by Bobby Timmons, lyric by Jon Hendricks

first chorus

Ev'ry mornin' finds me moanin' (yes, Lord)
'cause of all the trouble I see, (yes, Lord)
life's a losin' gamble to me, (yes, Lord)
cares and woes have got me moanin'. (yes, Lord)

Ev'ry evenin' finds me moanin' (yes, Lord)
I'm alone and cryin' the blues, (yes, Lord)
I'm so tired of payin' these dues. (yes, Lord)
Ev'rybody knows I'm moanin'. (yes, Lord)

Lord I spend plenty of days and nights
alone with my grief, (alone with my grief)
and I pray, really 'n' truly pray,
somebody will come and bring me relief.

Ev'ry mornin' finds me moanin' (yes, Lord)
'cause of all the trouble I see, (yes, Lord)
life's a losin' gamble to me, (yes, Lord)
cares and woes have got me moanin'. (yes, Lord)

last chorus

Ev'ry mornin' finds me moanin' (yes, Lord)
'cause of all the trouble I see, (yes, Lord)
life's a losin' gamble to me, (yes, Lord)
cares and woes have got me moanin'. (yes, Lord)

Ev'ry evenin' finds me moanin' (yes, Lord)
I'm alone and cryin' the blues, (yes, Lord)
I'm so tired of payin' these dues. (yes, Lord)
Ev'rybody knows I'm moanin'. (yes, Lord)

Lord I spend plenty of days and nights
alone with my grief, (alone with my grief)
and I pray, really 'n' truly pray,
somebody will come and bring me relief.

coda

Ev'ry evenin' finds me moanin' (yes, Lord)
I'm alone and cryin' the blues, (yes, Lord)
I'm so tired of payin' these dues. (yes, Lord)
Ev'rybody knows I'm moanin'. (yes, Lord)

Lord, I try, really and truly try,
to find some relief. (find some relief)
Lord, I spend plenty of days and nights
alone with my grief. (alone with my grief)
Lord, I pray, really and truly pray,
to find some relief.
Yes, Lord.

MY LITTLE SHERRI
music by Charlie Rouse, lyric by Ben Sidran

[1] I wanna go and be a movie star,
I want to ride in a big car looking like a million.
I want to go and get to Hollywood,
go while the going is still good.
But nothing there can take the place of you,
I got to tell you, you really got me skipping.

[2] I got the offer just the other day,
it came from Quincy in L.A., he's looking for a player.
Got in the car and went to your front door,
there's something for me, I know it.
No one nowhere can take the place of you,
I got to tell you, you really got me skipping.

[3] There's something fine about your whole design,
there's something real in your appeal.
They don't have that in L.A.
There's something good about your neighborhood,
I think it's you and you know it.
No one nowhere can take the place of you,
no one can do the things that you can do,
my little Sherri, I'm in love with you.
I got to tell you, you really got me skipping, skip on!

NEVER BEEN IN LOVE
music by Tadd Dameron, lyric by Irving Reid

verse: I was wise beyond my years,
laughed no laughs and cried no tears.
Love was just a word, an absurdity,
love could never happen to me.

chorus

Never been in love,
never been in love,
never been in love with anyone.

Hardly spoke of love,
made a joke of love.
Rugged individual,
I passed it by, without a try.

Never touched a hand
that could touch my hand,
no one's kiss left mem'ries in my heart.
I was too smart.

Life was brightly dull,
one exciting lull,
Then his/her smile reached out to me
and lit the place, and changed my face.

Sentimental, sweet and gentle, happy, I could cry.
All at once I'm as gentle as a lamb.
Never been in love but now I am.

OH! GEE!
music and lyric by Matthew Gee

[1] Oh! Gee! I'm in misery,
my cool fine baby has taken a powder on me.
Without a word, he/she upped and left,
and now I'm watchin' television by myself.
No word he/she was leavin'
now I am grievin' about my sweet little baby,
I'm nearly crazy.

[2] Oh! Gee! Just what could it be
that made my sweetie turn the cooler on me?
He/she left me flat, and that is that,
but still I'd like to have my lovin' baby back.
He/she knows how to please me,
somebody help me please to find my baby,
my pretty baby.

bridge
He/she would never be content out there all alone
and I would gladly take him/her back
if he/she would only phone. I'm screamin',

[3] Oh! Gee! Just what could it be,
that made my baby turn a damper on me?
He/she told his/her friends that we were through,
I sure would like to ask that ⎧man just⎫ what did I do
                                ⎩woman ⎭
to make him/her desert me, Oh! Gee!
It hurt me when I lost my baby,
I'm nearly crazy.

last bridge
He/she would never be content out there all alone
and I would gladly take him/her back
if he/she would only phone. I'm screamin',

[4] Oh Gee! Why I didn't see
that one day this would ever happen to me.
He/she told his/her friends that we were through,
I sure would like to ask that ⎧man just⎫ what did I do
                                ⎩woman ⎭
to make him/her desert me. Oh! Gee!
It hurt me when I lost my baby,

coda
my pretty baby, Oh! Gee!
Just what could it be, Oh! Gee!

Copyright © 1961 (renewed 1989) Twenty-Eighth Street Music

ONE DREAM GONE
music by Curtis Fuller, lyric by Fleurine

One dream gone, one more chapter closed,
one illusion I lost, yet I go on.
I know that one day I'll dream again,
one fine day I'll open my heart
and give love to one.

For now I live, one deception's clear,
but I won't let it change my mood, my dear.
For you were the one who really lost,
you lost me.

coda
you lost me, me.

Copyright © 1961 (renewed 1989), 1995 Second Floor Music

ONE FINE DAY
music by Ray Bryant, lyric by L. Aziza Miller

Your smile is my joy and laughter,
you're the one I knew my heart was after.
My feelings were an indigo blue
until one fine day I met you.

The look in your eyes so tender,
ev'ry kiss, a silent wish remembered.
Never had a clue my lonely days were all through
until one fine day I met you.

You've given me a new reason to sing.
Gone away the tears, I welcome the sun
as we share our love together as one.

Your touch is my greatest pleasure,
you're the miracle that my heart treasures.
When you're loving me, there's no place I'd rather be
than inside your arms completely.
Ev'ry kiss, a wish remembered
and ev'ry touch, so much, my love surrenders.
first time
Explore as love unfolds!
last time (coda)
Let body mind and soul
explore as love unfolds.
And when the poets speak of love, they'll all say
it happened one fine day.

Copyright © 1956 (renewed 1984), 1996 Second Floor Music

ONE HEART'S DREAM
music by Rodgers Grant, lyric by Catherine Whitney

I heard that love may not always last
but our love could live forevermore
if only you would tell me just one time
that our love, which was true bliss,
had started with our first kiss.

But now I know hearts can lose their way
and love may sometimes go astray.
We know that love is magic,
it's like a dream lost in a mem'ry,
but our love is a gift from the heart.

Although you know love is always near
it takes us to places far away.
If you and I could just feel the same way
we did when we had first met,
the day we'll never forget.

You may not see what you hope to see
when love seems very far away.
Just remember that your love will return
just like a haunting daydream,
for your love is a gift from your heart.

Copyright © 1994, 1997 Second Floor Music

ORANGE BLOSSOMS IN SUMMERTIME
music by Curtis Lundy, lyric by Kurt Elling

When winter is on again,
fragrance ends
and the withered leaves
drift down from the dying trees
as they find release.
But I'll remember it:
the sweet perfume of
orange blossoms in summertime.

And when we are far apart
and my heart
feels a winter chill,
I've got to lay down and cry,
but I know, by and by,
that I'll remember it:
the sweet perfume of
orange blossoms in summertime.

Copyright © 1983, 1995 Second Floor Music

OUR LOVE REMAINS
music by Robert Watson and Pamela Baskin-Watson,
lyric by Pamela Baskin-Watson

Looking back on the years,
on the pain and the tears
that would fall, through it all,
our love remains.

People change, people grow,
we're no diff'rent, this we know,
but one thing stays the same,
our love remains.

Angry times, we've been through angry times
that led us to something new,
anger ends in making love.
We build our life on love to make it through,
only love gets us through

all those times we're apart.
Building dreams and planning schemes
we hope will grow, it's good to know
our love remains.

last time
our love remains,
our love remains.

Copyright © 1986, 1989 Second Floor Music

RHYME OF SPRING
music by Kenny Dorham, lyric by Meredith d'Ambrosio

As winter falls away,
you heed the call to play
and stroll along the way hiding from the moonlight.
It seems so real. You dream
of stealing a kiss; isn't this what you miss?
Loving hearts will sing
their rhyme of spring
and celebrate their time of mating.

Beneath a starry sky
love will intensify.
There's something you may spy in the atmosphere now.
It's clear that spring is here.
You're lost in the midst of a passionate kiss
till the moon descends.
So soon love ends.
It all depends on spring.
Who knows what the wind will bring?

Copyright © 1959 (renewed 1987), 1999 Second Floor Music

SEA BREEZE
music and lyric by Jon Burr

By the sea, so easy,
clear blue sky and breezy.
It's a feeling like a symphony in motion,
majesty in the sky and the ocean.

You and I, good weather,
on the sand together,
comes a moment all our cares just melt away.
Once more a perfect day.

SOFT AND FURRY
music by Johnny Griffin, lyric by Eddie Jefferson

I can say
that soft and furry
is just what she is,
and I'm not meaning to be naive.
She's soft and furry
when she's in my arms,
there's cause for alarm, it's love.

Yes, sir-ee,
she cuddles near me
so she can cheer me,
I feel like hollerin', "Yes indeed!"
That soft and furry
is just what she is,
as long as I live she's mine.

With the world all up in arms
there's nothing, no nothing, I look forward to.
But I know, dear, we're together,
there's no time to be blue.

I'm in love, we've got each other,
we'll never bother
about a rocketship to the moon.
We're both in heaven,
she's furry and soft
and that isn't all, she's mine.

SOFT WINDS
music by Fletcher Henderson, lyric by Fred Royal

{1} Soft winds whisper
sweet words to my love,
soft winds tell him/her
the dreams I'm dreaming of;
he's/she's gone too long
out on the blue sea,
find him/her, soft winds
and bring him/her back home to me.

{2} Blow, blow soft winds,
out on the blue sea,
tell him/her, soft winds,
I'm sad and lonely;
since he/she left me,
my heart is empty,
blow, blow soft winds
and bring him/her back home to me.

A SOMETHING IN A SUMMER'S DAY
*music by Kirk Nurock, lyric adapted from a poem by Emily Dickinson
(XII: Psalm Of The Day [from Nature])*

A something in a summer's day,
as slow her candles burn away.
A something in a summer's noon,
an azure depth, a wordless tune,
and still within a summer's night
a something so transporting bright,
I veil my too inspecting face,
lest such a subtle, shimm'ring grace
flutter too far for me.

The wizard-fingers never rest,
the purple brook within the breast
still chafes its narrow bed;
still rears the East her amber flag,
guides still the sun along the crag,
his caravan of red,
and still within a summer's night
a something so transporting bright,
I veil my too inspecting face,
lest such a subtle, shimm'ring grace
flutter too far for me.

last time
transcending ecstasy,
flutter too far for me.

SOMETIME AGO
music and lyric by Sergio Mihanovich

Life began when you came,
sometime ago,
there was love in the game
sometime ago.
So unconventional you and me
and so essentially young and free.

We were both very smart
until the end,
little girl/boy with no heart
I would pretend,
now I'm discovering
as I'm recovering
love wasn't really just a game,
but we're the only ones to blame.

Copyright © 1963 (renewed 1991) Second Floor Music

STRAIGHT AHEAD
music by Mal Waldron, lyric by Abbey Lincoln

Straight ahead the road keeps winding,
narrow, wet and dimly lit,
vainly looking for a crossroad
where a weary soul can sit.

Lost and needing some directions,
dodging ruts along the way,
bumpy road confuse a body,
lead a trusting soul astray.

For some the road is smooth and easy,
trav'lin' high without a care.
But if you got to use the backroads,
straight ahead can lead nowhere.

So on this road you got a problem
getting where you want to go,
speed limits almost down to nothing,
straight ahead but awful slow.

Copyright © 1961 (renewed 1989) Second Floor Music

SWEET AND TRUE
music by Curtis Fuller, lyric by Catherine Whitney

In the scheme of things,
when you're looking for love
and you wonder
if you'll ever find love,
just let it go, it will find you,
just see it through
and let your heart sing its love song.

Then one lucky day,
though it's hard to believe,
in walks love
and your loneliness leaves.
Enjoy the glow, joy of the soul,
all your desires unfolding now, so sweet and true.

coda
You found love sweet and true.

Copyright © 1979, 1984, 1996 Second Floor Music

THAT MAGIC RAPTURE
music by Harold Land, lyric by Meredith d'Ambrosio

I thought my heart
would never capture
the joy of spring;
that magic rapture.

I breathed a sigh. I could fly
as high as the sky
just as you wandered by,
and knew on that morn
I loved you before I was born.

coda
That magic rapture.

Copyright © 1978, 1999 Second Floor Music

THERE'S NO MORE BLUE TIME
music by Tadd Dameron, lyric by Georgie Fame

[1] In no condition to play my part
ever since you left and broke my heart.
My position is decidedly unsure,
and now I find I can't cope anymore.
I'm heading for a real blue time
'cause I can't get you out of my mind.

[2] Looking for action around the scene,
trying to forget what might have been.
Satisfaction never seems to come my way,
alas, and now I go from day to day
try'n' hard to lose these timeless blues.
I'm resigned to a very blue time.

[3] I've turned the corner, I'm going straight,
got you in my sights and just can't wait.
Oh, my dear, we won't spend any time apart
since you somehow have soothed my aching heart.
I've said goodbye to my blue time,
I'm real gone and I hope you don't mind
'cause I know from now on ev'rything will be fine.
There's no more blue time.

TOMORROW
music and lyric by Lonnie Hillyer

Tho' yesterday's dreams have all faded
and you seem to want me no more,
I cry not, I sigh not,
tomorrow is just 'cross the dawn.

I'll wake up and start out a new day,
a day filled with promise of love.
I'll stand strong; before long
someone may come.

Now watching the dawn is like
seeing a miracle
unfolding before my eyes.
It heightens and brightens with such ecstasy,
like you it mystifies me.

So gladly I'll greet its arrival,
I'll put on my very best self.
I'll cry not 'cause I've got
tomorrow and it's 'cross the dawn, it's coming on.

TWISTED
music by Wardell Gray, lyric by Annie Ross

[1] My analyst told me
that I was right out of my head,
the way he described it,
he said I'd be better dead than live.
I didn't listen to his jive,
I knew all along that he was all wrong,
and I knew that he thought
I was crazy, but I'm not, oh no.

[2] My analyst told me
that I was right out of my head,
he said I'd need treatment
but I'm not that eas'ly led.
He said I was the type that was most inclined
when out of his sight to be out of my mind,
and he thought I was nuts,
no more ifs or ands or buts, oh no.

1st solo chorus:
They say as a child
I appeared a little bit wild with all my crazy ideas,
but I knew what was happ'nin',
I knew I was a genius.
What's so strange
if you know that you're a wizard at three?
I knew that this was meant for me.

2nd solo chorus:
I heard little children were supposed to sleep tight,
that's why I drank a fifth of vodka one night.
My parents got frantic, didn't know what to do,
but I saw some crazy scenes before I came to.
Now, do you think I was crazy?
I may have been only three but I was swingin'!

3rd solo chorus:
They all laughed at A. Graham Bell,
they all laughed at Edison and also at Einstein,
so why should I feel sorry if they just
couldn't understand the reasoning and the logic
that went on in my head.
I had a brain, it was insane,
so I just let them laugh at me
when I refused to ride on all those double-decker buses
all because there was no driver on the top.

[3] My analyst told me
that I was right out of my head,
the way he described it,
he said I'd be better dead than live.
I didn't listen to his jive,
I knew all along that he was all wrong,
and I knew that he thought
I was crazy, but I'm not, oh no.

[4] My analyst told me
that I was right out of my head,
but I said "Dear Doctor,
I think that it's you instead,"
'cause I have got a thing that's unique and new.
It proves that I'll have the last laugh on you,
'cause instead of one head,

coda
huh, huh, huh, I got two.
And you know two heads are better than one.

TWO REFLECT AS ONE
music by Michael Cochrane, lyric by Cheryl Pyle

Figures
yearning,
spin like fall leaves turning.
Quietly dancing
duo,
shaded evening glow,
in the branch-like shadows
ghostly
touch the full moon closely,
expressions glisten
under
sky lit indigo.

Circling patterns, graceful
steps so old yet new,
watch as distant partners
soon become the waltzing me and you,

the faces
telling
silently love's dwelling.
Our lips are wordless,
smiling,
in first rays of sun,
two reflect as one.

THE UNDERDOG
music by Al Cohn, lyric by Dave Frishberg

Here I go again,
about to drop another bundle
on the underdog, the underdog.
Isn't it a shame, but that's the kind of game I play.

People think it's funny
if they see you've got your money
on the clown. When the chips are down,
and when your side gets outclassed
they say "Nice guys wind up last."

But there's a strange satisfaction,
when you're putting all your action
on the underdog, the underdog,
even when you know the odds can never go your way,

'cause fav'rites don't always win.
That long shot may come in, who can say?
And sooner or later,
you know ev'ry underdog will have his day.

interlude
You figure the odds, you pick and you choose,
some got to win, and some got to lose.
But know ev'ry underdog will have his day.

WARM BLUE STREAM
music by Sara Cassey, lyric by Dotty Wayne

Go my love, go my love,
like ripples in a warm blue stream.
Yes, flow my love, flow my love,
and I will follow in a dream.

Hazy now, lazy now,
and like a warm blue stream at play.
Ah, madly now, gladly now,
your love has carried me away.

And as I'm floating in space,
I feel your embrace
as sweet as a rose upon a vine.
And then I hear thunder
and at last you are mine
and never will I let you,
oh, how could I let you,
never will I let you go.

Ah, but go my love, go my love,
like ripples in a warm blue stream.
Yes, flow my love, flow my love,
and I will follow in a dream.

last time
Your love is like a warm blue stream.

WE NEVER KISSED
music and lyric by Melba Liston

Once I lived in a gay world
of laughter and fortune and fame.
You were part of this mad whirl
but we never kissed, what a shame.

Soon romances got started,
so diff'rent my old world became.
You found a love and departed
and we never kissed, what a shame.

Too late, I dreamed of your gentle eyes,
your voice, your smile and your touch.
Too late, I learned to whom my heart cries,
"My love, I need you so much."

Now I live in a gray world
and I've only myself to blame,
'cause you were part of my gay world
and we never kissed, what a shame.

WE'RE ALL THROUGH
music and lyric by Ruby Braff

We're all through,
yes we're done.
We gave our all and it was a ball.
Let's go home.

No more time,
you've been sublime,
really it is true
we must say good night to you.
Ciao and shalom,
we're going home,
we're all through.

Copyright © 1997 Twenty-Eighth Street Music

WHEN WE MEET AGAIN
music by Scott Whitfield, lyric by Michael Andrew

Now it's time to say goodbye, my love,
but there's no need to cry, my love.
Let's just hope time hurries by, my love,
until we meet again.

Darling, while I'm far away from you here,
I'll think of you each day of the year.
Now there's nothing left to say to you, dear,
until the moment when you can call.

I'll have all the things I'll miss,
your tender kiss, what bliss.
I promised I would never let you go,
and we'd never say goodbye.

Now it's not for us to know, my love,
what the fates will show, my love,
but there's one thing that is clear,
I'll see you, dear, so have no fear.
'Cause I know we'll be together then,
when we meet again.

last time
'Til then, I'll see you when we meet again.

Copyright © 1993, 1995 Twenty-Eighth Street Music and Minor Second Music

WHEN WE'RE ALONE
music by Clifford Brown, lyric by Michael Stillman

I know now (I didn't know then),
I know the way you stumble deep into my heart
whispering "Uh-oh!" my love,
you say my name, and I'm in trouble again.
And when we dance I know how (I never know when)
my old defenses crumble! You can be so smart,
whispering "Uh-oh!" my love,
I'm just a wall reduced to rubble again!

When we're alone I'm feelin' so rare,
the way you dare to treasure me!
And I'll be there
because you're there to pleasure me!
I see your hair full of the full moonlight,
and in the night you're like a dream
brighter than springtime!

And in my dreams I know now, as I awaken,
if I should toss and tumble (This is the best part!)
whispering "Uh-oh!" my love,
    first time
I'm so in love I'm seeing double again!
    last time (second measure of coda)
you take my hand and whisper "Uh-oh!" my love,
you hold me close and whisper "Uh-oh!" my love,
you say my name and I'm in trouble!

Copyright © 1956 (renewed 1984), 1998 Second Floor Music

WHO'S BEEN LOVIN' YOU?
music by Milton Sealey, lyric by L. Aziza Miller

"Who's been loving you?"
constantly I ask myself.
Feeling kind of blue,
have you found somebody else?
Does it have to end,
how can I trust love again?
You've got me confused.
Are we really through?
Who's been loving you?

Trying to forget
hasn't been an easy task.
Friends are telling me
that I'm living in the past.
I just can't believe
you're not coming home to me.
Nothing I can do.
Feeling kind of blue.
Who's been loving you?
coda
Who's been loving you?
Who's been loving you?

Copyright © 1990, 1997 Second Floor Music and Twenty-Eighth Street Music

WHY DO I STILL DREAM OF YOU?
music and lyric by Meredith d'Ambrosio

Why do I still dream of you?
Many years ago we parted,
and with ev'ry dream your voice is
heard sending unforgotten words
through my heart. I wonder

if, in all the years gone by,
while you slumber, you have felt me
smiling as I wander by your bed,
barely whisp'ring my plea
that we never say goodbye.

Copyright © 1996 Second Floor Music

WITHOUT REASON, WITHOUT RHYME
music and lyric by Meredith d'Ambrosio

I dove into love as if it were the sea.
Not a thing could keep me from you,
caught in love's sweet mystery.

And I believed
that the way to my heart's desire
was to banish all my fears.
I could set your soul on fire.

I barely recall the rapture in your voice,
so conspicuous by its absence.
How it made my heart rejoice.

But that was long ago in another time.
I would do it all again
through the gladness, through the pain,
without reason, without rhyme.

Copyright © 1997 Second Floor Music

WITHOUT YOU
music by Renee Rosnes, lyric by Shelley Brown

In your eyes, shines the moon,
in your hands, rest the stars,
with your kiss I have found eternity.

Without you, there is darkness,
with your smile, comes the light
and the stars fill the night.

In your eyes, shines my love,
in your hands, rests my heart.
If you asked, I'd be yours
'til the moon fades away,
'til the stars close their eyes
and time stands still.

Copyright © 1989, 2000 Second Floor Music

YOU ARE MINE
music and lyric by Norman Simmons

Infinite mystery of love,
you are mine;
I feel your presence come alive
here inside;
I'll protect you from harm,
from the day you are born,
in my arms, in my arms,
you'll be safe in my arms.

You are the wonder of my world,
you are mine;
mine to be loved until the ending of time;
from one moment of love
you're my gift from above.
You're my prayer, you're my life,
you're my own, you're divine,
you are mine.

Copyright © 1985 Second Floor Music

YOU KNOW WHO!
music and lyric by Bertha Hope

When you are lonely and blue,
don't know what to do,
cry awhile.
When things are lookin' rough,
and you're not so tough,
sigh awhile.

When you're thinkin' it through,
be good to the only one who
was there to care and pay your share of dues,
you know who! I mean you.

Now when your future looks bleak,
you have a mean streak,
sit awhile.
Just take a look around
and calm yourself down,
rest awhile.

Then depend on the one
you know who gets the work done,
no doubt, no fear, get in gear, do you hear?
You know who! I mean you.

last time
You know who! I mean you!

Copyright © 1989 Second Floor Music

YOU NEVER MISS THE WATER TILL THE WELL RUNS DRY
music and lyric by Lucky Thompson

Yes, baby, when you left me, you left me low and blue,
you said that you were going to get somebody new.
But baby, take this with you to remember by and by:
you never miss the water till the well runs dry.

You came home ev'ry morning at three or half past four,
I'd ask where have you been
and you'd leave and slam the door.
But baby, take this with you to remember by and by:
you never miss the water till the well runs dry.

Sometimes the grass seems greener on the other side
but all the other guy wants is to take you for a ride.
He'll tell you many sweet things, things you like to hear,
when you are broke, this ain't no joke,
he'll say goodbye, my dear.

So go on where you're going, and have yourself a ball,
'cause you're the one who's losing,
I'll be there when you fall.
But baby, take this with you to remember by and by:
you never miss the water till the well runs dry.

Copyright © 1978 Second Floor Music

YOU'LL ALWAYS BE THE ONE I LOVE
music and lyric by Gigi Gryce

I never knew
I could love you the way I do,
for my heart stands still,
whenever you are near, I'm thrilled.

My love for you
is a love that is deep and true.
Never let us part,
you satisfy my lonely heart.

The touch of your lips whenever we kiss
holds me under the spell of your charms.
How can I escape this feeling of bliss
that entangles me in your arms?

It's plain to see
there is no other one for me.
You're my star above,
you'll always be the one I love.

Copyright © 1955 (renewed 1984) Twenty-Eighth Street Music

YOU'RE MY ALTER EGO
music by James Williams, lyric by Pamela Baskin-Watson

I'll hear a tune
and begin to think of you,
you're on my mind 'most all the time.
I'll start to dream
and then all at once it seems,
you will appear before my eyes.

Who'd ever think
that a smile would capture me,
turning my world so far around.
Sharing my life
and fulfilling all my needs,
I'm holding on to what I've found.

Falling in love
has a way of making you
see only what you want to see.
I'll take a chance
on the things I see in you
and hope you'll take a chance on me.

When we're as one,
I become a part of you
and you become a part of me.
It feels so right,
I know God is blessing us
with all the love we'll ever need.

coda
I love you so,
you're my alter ego, don't
ever let me go.
My life is yours,
I'll be what you want me to
be, just let me know.
I love you so,
you're my alter ego, don't
ever let me go.

Copyright © 1982, 1983 Second Floor Music

HELPFUL HINTS

How to benefit the most from *Sing JAZZ!*

The publisher and editor of *Sing JAZZ!* have taken great care to include a useful array of tools to help you get the most from this book.

The **contents** on pages 4 and 5 lists all selections by vocal title, along with the composers and lyricists. If a song is known by a different title as an instrumental selection, that title is included as well. As an aid in selecting repertoire, we have also included recording artists. More can be found in the discography.

The **vocal lead sheets** are on pages 6-121.

The Lyrics Alone. The lyrics of each song are printed separately on pages 122-143. Reading and studying the texts of songs separately from the music are vital tools in selecting material and developing a unique interpretive approach. The performance of vocal jazz is a highly personalized art form. When developing an interpretive approach to a new song, many singers may find it useful to simply speak the lyrics, apart from the melody, to find their subtleties, accents and emotional nuances. The lyrics in this section are divided into lines that conform to the musical phrasing.

This **helpful hints** section (pages 144-149) offers further insights into the music.

The **glossary** (page 151) explains the music notation and many of the terms used in the lead sheets. A glance through it will help you in reading the music.

There are brief biographies of **the people** who wrote the music in this book, starting on page 154.

The **discography** on pages 164-169 includes listings of current and historically important recordings of many of the songs, including the instrumental versions. Of course, new recordings and artists appear all the time, so the list is not complete. Try to listen to many recordings: listening to another artist's interpretation can give you new insights into the music and text. When the recording happens to be made by the lyricist (as is the case here with Meredith d'Ambrosio, Vanessa Rubin and Fleurine, for instance), you may discover additional interpretive nuances.

Indexes. We've included an index arranged by composer (page 170) and one arranged by lyricist (page 172), so you can quickly locate titles by your favorite writers.

A listing of songs according to **tempo** is included on page 176. This resource is intended to help you identify just the right song to add to a performance set and your repertoire. You can quickly find a jazz waltz, a bossa, an unusual time signature like 5/4, or a ballad, for example.

We hope this volume will help vocalists and instrumentalists select appropriate and interesting songs for study and to include in their working repertoire. And remember, when you learn a song, try to adapt it flexibly to your individual singing style. Jazz singing is an idiom built upon innovation as well as firm musical skills.

Notes on using the lead sheets

All lead sheets in *Sing JAZZ!* incorporate a variety of notations and features, some standard to lead sheet format, others unique to this book. Like all lead sheets, they provide the melody, lyric and chord progression. Additionally, note the following:

If the lyric version has been recorded, a **recording credit** is shown above the composition title. Other recordings, if any, will be detailed in the discography section.

Where the composition was originally an instrumental, and a lyric was later added, the **instrumental title** is shown under the title of the vocal version.

Often the original instrumental keys have been changed so the songs are in keys which are friendly to medium-range voices. The vocal lead sheet **key** of each song is indicated in the top left corner; however, if a key identification isn't appropriate, the first chord symbol is used instead.

A **tempo/rhythmic "feel" indication**, such as medium swing, bossa, samba, or ballad, is on each lead sheet.

Rehearsal letters. On the most obvious level, these indications (Ⓐ, Ⓑ, etc.) offer a convenient way for singers, coaches and instrumentalists to find and rehearse different sections of each song.

At the beginning of each line you will find **measure numbers** (also called bar numbers) as an aid in rehearsing as well as interpretive planning and other purposes.

Solo sections (for improvising) are defined with measure numbers shown at the end of the melody [for example, *to solos (1-32)*]. These measure numbers identify the sections that are suggested for instrumental solos, for scat singing, for freer improvisation around the text or for other interpretive approaches.

Indications of **rhythmic hits** are noted above or sometimes below the musical staff. They are designed to clarify rhythmic emphasis for the rhythm section or accompaniment instruments. You'll find these hints on where to place the strong accents will help make a song come alive, as well as provide authenticity to a song that has been known previously only as an instrumental.

Please review the **glossary** (page 151) for additional definitions and for clarification of the notation used in this book.

INTRODUCTIONS

In determining what introduction to use for a song, the general tendency or "rule of thumb" is to try the last four measures of the piece as an introduction. You also might be able to use a standard I–VI–II–V7 turn-around progression, an entirely different set of chords, or sometimes just an arpeggio set-up on one particular chord.

However, the first two songs in this book were written with introductions as integral elements (built-in introductions). *Another Time, Another Place* utilizes a built-in ostinato introduction. This bass line introduction (**Intro**) is also the accompaniment to the melody, as indicated. The introduction sets up the song and introduces the background used at letter Ⓐ. Lyricist Pam Watson's original concept for the song starts with a whisper on the words "make time stand still" and that's how the lead sheet is presented here. When Kevin Mahogany recorded the song, he began singing at letter Ⓐ and used the whisper effect at the end of the song. This is an example of how individual interpretation can shape an arrangement.

This song is a good example of a layered effect, in that the bass line begins the song, chords enter after the bass line introduction, then the melody with lyrics begins at letter Ⓐ. The interlude at letter Ⓒ restates the chord patterns used in the beginning of the piece. In this case, the solo section reference (defining a solo chorus) is from measures 37-59 or sections Ⓓ, Ⓔ, and Ⓕ (they are the same as sections Ⓐ, Ⓑ, and Ⓒ). After the solos, *D.S.* indicates a return to the Interlude (at the sign 𝄋) followed by the **Coda** and the vamp. This is a great arrangement just as written: it includes an introduction, an interlude between choruses to set up the solo sections, and it has a written-out ending.

All My Love, Especially For You is another example of a song with a built-in introduction. This song was recorded instrumentally as an orchestrated big-band arrangement. I find this arrangement works just as well for a piano introduction and is an excellent way to set the song up for the singer. Certainly, other types of arrangements may be written for this song that could lend a variety of creative approaches.

Life's Mosaic has a built-in introduction and ending which was written as part of the composition.

Songs that contain built-in introductions with an ostinato type of intro include *I'll Remember Love* and *You Know Who! I'll Remember Love* utilizes an ostinato four-measure introduction that sets up the piece harmonically, as well as providing a groove at the beginning. The same type of introduction can be seen in *You Know Who!*

Songs with built-in introductions organized by type of intro:

Ostinato type intro:
Another Time, Another Place (medium swing): 4-measure repeating bass line
I'll Remember Love (medium swing): repeating 2-measure bass line and counter-melody
Like An Old Song (5/4 time): repeating 2-measure rhythmic counter-melody
Long As You're Living (5/4 time): entire blues bass line
Meant To Be! (medium swing): 8-measure bass line
Our Love Remains (slow Latin): 2-measure bass line with changing harmony
Sea Breeze (Latin-samba): 8-measure counter-melody
That Magic Rapture (medium Latin): 8-measure bass line

Ending used as intro:
Honeydo (medium swing)
It's All In The Mind (medium swing)
The Man With The Magic (3/4 time)

The third song in the book, *Alone Again*, like many other ballads or bossas, does not have a written beginning or ending. If it's performed as a ballad, the last four measures can be used as an instrumental introduction, or perhaps try just an introductory chord. When it's performed as a bossa, the introduction may again be the last four measures, or you could use the last two measures, repeated, making a four-bar repeated pattern to set up the bossa rhythmic feel. The singer and accompanist must determine the introduction that works best for them and for that particular song.

Many songs indicated as ballads may also be thought of and performed as bossa novas, depending on the concept and interpretation of the individual singer. Many ballads can become bossas by simply adopting a bossa nova tempo and rephrasing the melody and lyrics. Try both approaches to *Love And Deception* (page 56), and you'll see how creative rhythmic and melodic phrasing can alter the meaning of the lyric.

BLUES

Sing JAZZ! also includes a number of blues. This popular song form provides additional repertoire for the singer. It's also a good choice when inviting guest instrumental soloists to perform with you.

There are several variations of the blues in *Sing JAZZ!*: 12-bar; 16-bar; blues with a bridge; blues in 5/4 time signature, and others.

The typical blues consists of a 12-bar form. Usually when singing a blues, the vocalist will sing two complete choruses before "opening up" the song for instrumental and/or vocal solo choruses.

The famous Wardell Gray composition *Twisted*, with lyric by Annie Ross, is a great example of the blues as well as a superbly constructed solo. Annie Ross wrote a lyric to Wardell Gray's 12-bar blues melody and to the three choruses of his recorded tenor sax solo. This is a great addition to one's repertoire as well as a study piece in solo development and construction. This song may be performed using only the melody, then improvising on the blues changes, or by singing the melody and the entire solo section, as shown on pages 95-97.

Soft Winds, with the lyric, is always a 16-bar blues. When recorded instrumentally, sometimes measures 7-10 are eliminated and the song is

played as a 12-bar blues. A famous instrumental version, by Art Blakey and The Jazz Messengers on the "At The Cafe Bohemia, volume 1" recording, is done in the 12-bar format.

Oh! Gee! is a blues with an added bridge section. The 12-bar blues pattern is established at letters A and A1, and from there the song moves to an 8-measure bridge. *Oh! Gee!* uses a "rhythm" bridge followed by one more chorus of the blues (ⓒ). Generally, a "rhythm" bridge means to play the same changes as the bridge of the George and Ira Gershwin standard *I Got Rhythm*. Often, a blues with a bridge will include two choruses of the standard 12-bar blues changes and a bridge using "rhythm" changes, ending with another chorus of the 12-bar blues. This is a standard format for blues with a bridge, but it's not always the case, as sometimes completely different chord progressions are used for the bridge.

Long As You're Living is a blues in 5/4 time, giving you yet another opportunity to sing and/or play the blues in a different time signature and "feel." This song has two different melodies. The Ⓑ melody is derived from the bass line that is used as both the intro and under the Ⓐ melody. Each singer makes his or her own musical choices about arrangement and performance. Listen to some of the numerous artists who have recorded this song and see how their creative ideas have shaped their presentations. Abbey Lincoln sings the arrangement as is with no added solo sections; Judy Niemack begins with the Ⓑ melody; Claudia Acuña eliminates the intro, starting with Ⓐ then ending with Ⓑ.

Blues:
Chillin': 12-bar
Long As You're Living: 12-bar
My Little Sherri: variations (15-bar and 16-bar form)
Oh! Gee!: 12-bar with bridge
Soft Winds: 16-bar
There's No More Blue Time: 12-bar
Twisted: 12-bar

In The Lyrics Alone section, each melody blues chorus is numbered: [1], [2], etc.

BALLADS

Although most of the selections in this book have specific instructions for navigating from the beginning to the end (*D.S. al fine*, *D.C. al Coda*, etc.), we have intentionally left the instructions for ballads a little vague by omitting (in most cases) directions to return to the beginning after a solo section. Ballads are usually performed at a slow tempo, so repeating the whole form after the solos is often not practical. Instead, it's common for the vocalist to sing the entire song, return to the beginning for an instrumental solo (which could be half a chorus), after which the vocalist will come back in at the bridge and sing the remainder of the song to the end. This would be a two-chorus version. There may be situations in which the singer may decide to return to another section of the song (if not the bridge, maybe the last half), then continue to the end; or perhaps to sing only one chorus. Examples of performances with one chorus are Gloria Lynne's recording of *We Never Kissed* and *Straight Ahead,* as recorded by Abbey Lincoln. The version of *Straight Ahead* sung by Jeannie Lee, with Mal Waldron (the composer) on piano, is also a one-chorus performance, in a rubato tempo.

It's very important to decide what tempo you want for your performance. Sing a few bars, either out loud or silently to yourself, and try to establish a comfortable tempo that you can internalize. Set a metronome to match the tempo you have in your mind. Then you can use the metronome setting to calculate the length of a chorus. When you know how long one chorus is, you can plan your performance.

The formula. The top number of the time signature tells the number of beats per bar. Multiply the number of beats per bar by the number of bars in one chorus. Divide that answer by the metronome setting (M.M.). The resulting number to the left of the decimal point is the number of minutes per chorus. Calculate the number of additional seconds by multiplying the number to the right of the decimal point (the decimal fraction) by 60 (60 seconds per minute). For the exact timing of a chorus, combine the minutes and seconds. Use the chart below.

Get the following information: $\underline{\quad}$ $\underline{\quad}$ $\underline{\quad}$ *Then,*
beats/bar   bars/chorus   tempo (M.M.)

❶ $\dfrac{\quad}{\text{beats/bar}}$ X $\dfrac{\quad}{\text{bars/chorus}}$ = $\dfrac{\quad}{\text{beats/chorus}}$ ❷ $\dfrac{\quad}{\text{beats/chorus}}$ ÷ $\dfrac{\quad}{\text{tempo (M.M.)}}$ = $\dfrac{\quad}{\text{duration (decimal minutes)}}$

Convert to minutes and seconds: the integer (whole number) is the number of whole minutes. Then change the decimal minutes to seconds:

❸ $\dfrac{\quad}{\text{decimal fraction}}$ x 60 (seconds/minute) = $\dfrac{\quad}{\text{number of seconds}}$

❹ $\dfrac{\quad}{\text{minutes}}$ + $\dfrac{\quad}{\text{seconds}}$ = total duration of 1 chorus

For example, in 4/4 time, if a chorus is 32 bars and your tempo is 68 beats per minute:
❶ 4 beats per bar x 32 bars = 128 beats per chorus
❷ 128 ÷ 68 M.M. = 1.88 decimal minutes
❸ .88 x 60 seconds = 52.8 seconds
❹ Add minutes and seconds and round off:
   1 minute 53 seconds per chorus.

One chorus of *The Love We Had Yesterday*, a 32-measure ballad in 4/4 time played at ♩ = 48, will take 2 minutes 40 seconds. Adding a one chorus piano solo will double the playing time (5:20). You may not want to perform another complete chorus (the song would be 8 minutes long). To shorten your performance, you could come in at the bridge after the piano solo (a total of 6:40). However, you'd have to do some planning because the turn-around chords at the end of the solo section (measures 31-32) lead harmonically to letter Ⓐ, not to the bridge; also, there is a vocal pick-up before the bridge Ⓑ. So, in place of the F♯9sus chord in measure 32, you would play and sing the bar before Ⓑ.

Rubato sections will, of course, increase the performance time.

You must be the judge of your audience (or your recording time limit, or other pertinent factors) in deciding on your arrangements and performing strategies.

INTERPRETATION

Breathing Life Into The Songs

For those who are new to the idiom of vocal jazz—classical singers, pianist/accompanists, choral directors, singing teachers and other musicians— we would like to offer some insights on how to approach the lead sheets.

Jazz singing is an idiom imbued with creativity, flexibility and improvisation. It is important to learn the song as the composer wrote it, with the correct melody, rhythm and lyric. But after that, the singer should feel free to develop individual approaches in phrasing both the melody and the lyric.

Jazz singing is different from other kinds of singing, in that much of the emphasis is on the words, the sense of "inner time," and how the singer chooses to phrase the music. Often, that means taking a conversational approach instead of a purely vocal one. Remember, lead sheets are musical outlines—musical shorthand intended to be adapted and used flexibly in a variety of ways.

An examination of several approaches to *Never Been In Love* will demonstrate different ways to interpret the melody rhythmically. This song contains a verse, which introduces the story of the song, setting the mood. The tempo marking in the verse is "rubato," which suggests to "rob the time." Use the notated rhythm as an outline for an individual and unique conversational approach. The melody and lyric are written in a specific rhythm; however, varying the rhythm can be an extremely effective way to convey subtle inflections in meaning. It may help you in developing your own interpretation to speak the lyric apart from the melody and rhythm at first, in order to get in touch with what you want to communicate. Then begin singing the melody with your own conversational inflections and nuances.

In the rubato verse section, you can "say" or "speak" the words, using different emphases to vary the rhythm as outlined in the lead sheet. For example, in the first measure of the verse try different inflections: the words shown in bold type below imply more emphasis and a longer duration.

I was wise be-yond my **years**.

I was wise **be-yond my years**.

I was **wise** be-yond my years.

The following musical examples illustrate phrasing and rhythmic variations for the chorus, which would be performed in a ballad tempo (slow 4/4). These variations show different rhythmic possibilities within the first 8-measure phrase.

Variations 1 and 2 begin on beat one.

Never Been In Love
Music by Tadd Dameron
Lyric by Irving Reid
Copyright © 1978 TWENTY-EIGHTH STREET MUSIC

Variation 3 on the next page shows the lyric beginning on beat 4, using sixteenth notes. This suggests a more conversational approach.

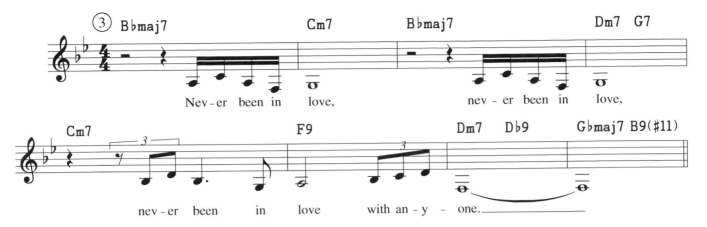

Variations 4 through 9 show other ways to rephrase and reshape the two-measure phrase "Never been in love" which is repeated throughout the chorus. Note the further rhythmic variations in these examples.

A careful listener will be quick to pick up on many variations that jazz singers make when interpreting melody and text. Here are a few more techniques that can be found in analyzing the interpretations of different artists.

Structural Changes

A lead sheet might present a song in the composer's original A-A-B-A (or A-B-A, etc.) structural format. In performance, there is no reason the singer cannot make structural decisions of his or her own, which might include:

• Allowing the instrumentalists to play the A section, then joining in at the B section or at another point that can be justified on interpretive grounds.

• Utilizing the melodic line as the vehicle for an improvised solo.

• Utilizing the last four measures of a song as an instrumental introduction to the A section. Or perhaps using the bridge as an intro—it is fine to experiment.

• Beginning with the B section, the bridge, or any other section of the song. Patti (of Tuck and Patti) begins the song *When We're Alone* in a rubato feel. She starts in measure 16 with the phrase containing the title of the song, "When we're alone," and sings through measure 24, "and in my dreams." She then sings the melody in a medium swing tempo from the beginning, after a guitar interlude. Although this lead sheet of *When We're Alone* (known instrumentally as *Joy Spring*) contains the rhythmic accents and hits and shows the turns (↝) that can be heard in Clifford Brown's original recording, the turns are optional for the singer.

Changes of Rhythm or Genre

• A jazz ballad could, with a subtle rhythmic shift, become a bossa or some other Latin beat, or even a medium or uptempo swing tune.

• Sometimes a song with a Latin feel can be effective performed with a swing feel, such as Mark Murphy's interpretation of *You're My Alter Ego*.

• A slow or medium swing number can be effective in a faster swing tempo. Listen to *There's No More Blue Time* as sung by Mark Murphy as an example.

You are limited only by your imagination. It is also helpful to solicit suggestions from your pianist and instrumentalists. Through such adaptive shifts, songs can take on a whole new character and tone.

Dynamics

The use of dynamics is a wonderful way to convey nuances of meaning and to display a greater emotional palette. In this book we have indicated general dynamic levels only for instrumental sections. Vocalists should make their own decisions about dynamic levels, in keeping with the story of the lyric.

Subtle Rephrasing and Reshaping of Text

This, of course, is where a jazz singer's artistry resides. It would be impossible to list all the interpretive wiles that jazz singers have applied to texts. Here are a few suggestions that might prove good starting points for singers exploring jazz for the first time:

• Break the text of longer phrases into shorter, more conversational units. An example of this may be seen in *Baby, I'm Coming Home* (page 13). The first phrase is rather long—four bars in length. By looking at the lyric alone (page 123), we see that the lyric can be divided into small units. Instead of thinking and singing the entire 4 bars, conceptualize smaller units so you can inject conversational inflections or nuances. Make sure that you are telling the story of the song, though, and not just singing separate phrases.

• *Heavenly!* (page 35) also has long musical phrases, but on the lyric page (128) we have broken these phrases into smaller units. This may give you ideas about where to breathe and how to phrase the musical lines.

• Speak the text of an introduction or verse or other section of the song before trying to sing it. *Never Been In Love* (see the musical examples on pages 148 and 149) includes a verse prior to letter Ⓐ. By speaking the lyrics first, you can make choices about how to phrase this section when singing it using a rubato approach.

• *That Magic Rapture* (page 92) has long phrases containing several measures of tied whole notes. In her recording, Meredith d'Ambrosio interprets these phrases effectively without the literal sustain of the whole notes.

• Betty Carter's unique personality shows through in her recording of *The Love We Had Yesterday*. Ms. Carter chose to phrase the melody and lyrics in an extreme delayed or back-phrased style.

Again, the choice of how to interpret a song is a matter of each singer's preference and artistic discretion.

Listen to other performers on instrumental and vocal recordings to find techniques that you might choose to add to your own repertoire of musical tools. If you listen and follow along with the lead sheets at the same time, it will immediately become clear to you that jazz singers and instrumentalists rarely feel obligated to adhere too closely or too precisely to the exact notated rhythms in the lead sheet (often even melody notes are reinterpreted). The objective is to make each song your own, while being mindful of each composition's original melody, harmony, rhythm, and lyric content.

There is much to be learned from listening to recordings by instrumentalists as well as vocalists. We have provided an extensive discography of instrumental and vocal recordings for your reference on page 164.

Using these lead sheets as foundations, find your own way to get the songs across while adapting them to your particular style and voice. The greatest jazz vocalists have always found ways to add their personal interpretations to the words and the music they've sung. It is our hope that, with **Sing JAZZ!**, you can add your own personal interpretation, something new and unique, to the ever-evolving art of vocal jazz!

Dr. Gloria Cooper

GLOSSARY

Included in some definitions are song titles, which illustrate the use (and often the first appearance) of the defined terms. Many terms are standard music notation terms that can be found in any music dictionary.

[1] in **The Lyrics Alone** section, the melody **blues** choruses are numbered *(Chillin')*

1-feel the underlying pulse is one beat per measure *(Don't Go)*

2-feel The underlying pulse of the music is in a half note rather than a walking 4-beat pulse (referred to as 4-feel). Unless labeled as 2-feel, the swing feeling will be understood to be 4-feel.

8va, 8vb indicates a passage to be played up an octave or down an octave, respectively

ad lib. *(ad libitum)* take liberties with what is written; improvise *(Another Time, Another Place)*

arpeggio play the notes of a chord separately and in succession.

(Bb) (F) **bass notes** circled note names, under or above the staff, indicate bass notes *(Ballad For Miles)*

bend ◡ bend the pitch *(Twisted)*

blues see page 146 for a discussion of the blues

bossa short for bossa nova; originally a Latin (Brazilian) style combining elements of samba and jazz

break, solo break a specified number of bars usually at the end of the melody before the beginning of a solo, where the rhythm section lays out; soloist improvises alone *(Beloved)*

, **breath mark** a short break, a pause *(Cup Of Life)*

bridge middle, contrasting section of the melody; the B section of an AABA form

ca. *(circa)* approximate, approximately

call and response Musical phrases played by one part are answered by another part. The response is optional. Two songs in this book *(Moanin'* and *I'll Remember Love)* have optional responses that could be sung by another singer or singers. Shown by small notes with lyric in parentheses.

chord symbols $\frac{Gb}{F}$ indicates a Gb triad with a bass note of F

[F7#5(#9)] **chord symbol in brackets** alternate or optional chord *(Beloved)*

(Gm) **chord symbol in parentheses** implied chord *(One Fine Day)*

chorus The main body of a composition (the basic form, not the introduction or the coda). "Take a chorus" means to improvise over the form of the song. The chord progression in the chorus is often repeated for solos. The *Another Time, Another Place* lead sheet shows two choruses: (A) - (C) (1 chorus) is the same as (D) - (F).

⊕ **Coda** an extended ending

comp an abbreviation for accompany *(I'll Remember Love)*

cue size notes (small notes) Either an optional vocal note or an instrumental accompaniment note. Also see double note, optional melody note *(Cup of Life)*.

delayed, **back-phrased style**, **laid back** melody notes are played or sung after the accompanying harmony has already been played

double note (see optional melody note) the preferred note is regular size, the optional note is small size and in parentheses *(Another Time, Another Place)*

down stems Down-stemmed melody notes are used for the second verse if it is rhythmically different than the first *(Christmas Morning In The Snow, The Coaster, Two Reflect As One)*.

D.C. *(da capo)* go back to the beginning

D.S. *(dal segno)* go back to the sign 𝄋

D.S. al Coda go back to the sign 𝄋, then at the mark ⊕ skip to the Coda

D.S. al fine (or *D.C. al fine*) go back to the sign 𝄋 (or to the beginning, if *D.C.*), play to the end

fall off ↘ let the pitch drop or fall after the melody note is sung *(Oh! Gee!)*

feel refers to the underlying rhythmic pulse. See 1-feel, 2-feel, 4-feel *(Another Time, Another Place; Heavenly!)*.

fill ⌐ Drums or instrumental fill - - - - - - ⌐ outlined solo space; improvise within the indicated area. During an instrumental fill the accompanying instruments improvise for a section. Can be optional.

fine marks the ending, or suggests one way to end the song; (⌢ *fine*) indicates the last note, ending note *(Another Time, Another Place)*

ghost notes (represented by x) are implied notes *(Chillin')*

grace notes optional vocal notes *(Garden In The Sand)*

hits see rhythmic hits

instrumental indicates that no lyrics are sung, the accompanying instruments play the notes *(The Man With The Magic)*

interlude usually an inserted instrumental section *(Another Time, Another Place)*

intro Introduction, played before the melody begins. In this book, a written introduction is usually an essential part of the composition. See the discussion on page 145.

key A friendly-to-medium-range-voice key has been selected for each song, often different from the original key. The *vocal lead sheet key* is indicated in the top left corner. If a key identification isn't appropriate, the first chord symbol is used instead.

layered Successive elements combine to create the complete texture. *Another Time, Another Place* is a good example of a layered effect, in that the bass line begins the song, chords enter after the bass line introduction, and the melody with lyric begins at letter Ⓐ.

lead sheet melody, chord symbols and lyric, not an arrangement

line breaks in **The Lyrics Alone** section, how the lyric is divided into lines reflecting the musical phrasing

lyric in parentheses optional words *(Another Time, Another Place; I'll Remember Love; Moanin')*

measure numbers (bar numbers) For rehearsal convenience, consecutive measure numbers are indicated at the start of each staff. Measure numbers do not reflect the form, as each measure is only counted once. Measure number references are used to indicate which measures define the solo sections: *solos (1-32)*.

 optional melody note shown small size, in parentheses in the vocal line. Sing the B♭ if you can't sing the F *(Another Time, Another Place)*. Also see double note.

ostinato a repeated rhythmic pattern

p4 chord made of perfect fourth intervals *(Warm Blue Stream)*

❜ pause a short break, or breath *(Without You)*

// grand pause, a definite break, longer pause *(Like An Old Song)*

pick-up notes that occur before the downbeat of the first complete measure of melody *(Twisted)*

pick-up to melody Ⓐ (or Ⓑ) **only** In the last bar of the last solo, the vocalist sings the pick-up to the melody.

rehearsal letters Ⓐ, Ⓑ, etc. used for convenience in rehearsing; also indicate different sections of the form

recording credit If the vocal version has been recorded, a recording credit will be indicated above the title. Other recordings, vocal and instrumental, can be found in the discography starting on page 164.

✗ repeat sign for one measure: repeat the previous measure *(Ballad For Miles)*

𝄎 repeat the previous 2 measures *(Sea Breeze)*

‖: :‖ repeat signs repeat the material between the repeat signs

repeat and fade play the indicated section several times, then fade out *(The Coaster)*

response as in call and response. Musical phrases played by one part are answered by another part. The response is optional. Two songs in this book *(Moanin'* and *I'll Remember Love)* have optional responses that could be sung by another singer or singers. Shown by small notes with lyric in parentheses.

 rest for the indicated number of bars; the rhythm section plays *(Like An Old Song, My Little Sherri)*

rhythm changes same chord structure as George & Ira Gershwin's 32-bar standard *I Got Rhythm*

rhythm section simile or **rhythm simile** The rhythm section (or piano/guitar) plays in the same manner as previously indicated; keep playing in a similar way *(Another Place, Another Time)*.

 **rhythmic hits** written usually above the staff, or sometimes below the staff, indicating harmonic or rhythmic patterns essential to the composition *(Another Place, Another Time)*

rit. (*ritard., ritardando*) indicates slowing of the tempo

rubato out of tempo, with elasticity

separate instrumental systems show the melody line and an instrumental line, usually the bass line *(The Coaster; Soft And Furry)*

simile continue in a similar manner

slashes / / / / show beat placement, usually implying additional accompaniment improvisation *(All My Love, Especially For You; The Gift Of Love; One Fine Day)*

 **slide** upward into the note *(Oh! Gee!)*

solo (improvise) for the indicated number of bars *(All My Love, Especially For You)*

Solos (Blues) solo on any mutually agreed upon blues progression *(Chillin')*

suggested embellishment optional notes suggested by the composer *(A Something In A Summer's Day)*

sus4-3 *(. . . Summer's Day)* the 4th resolves to the 3rd

tempo/rhythmic feel indications Suggested tempo approaches are shown above the time signatures. Style changes are shown in bold *(Twisted)*. Occasionally a metronomic meter marking is given *(Like An Old Song)*.

    ballad implies slow swing feeling, unless otherwise indicated

    swing either slow, medium, medium slow, medium up or uptempo

    Latin or more specific as bossa or samba

See the listing of songs by **tempo** and **style** on page 176.

turn (embellishment) Optional for vocalist. *(Another Time, Another Place; That Magic Rapture; When We're Alone)*

turn-around chords at the end of one section that provide a transition into the next section, sometimes shown in parentheses *(Chillin')*

tutti accompaniment plays the melody with the voice *(Honeydo)*

vamp keep repeating until cued to go to next section or fade out, or end *(Another Time, Another Place)*

verse an added melody with lyric that introduces and sets up the main melody *(Never Been In Love)*

About Dr. Gloria Cooper

Dr. Gloria Cooper, an impressive jazz pianist and vocalist who is also an esteemed academician, has had a lengthy and fruitful career as both a performer and an educator.

Cooper began piano studies at age five and soon studied voice. She eventually attended the University of Missouri, where she received her bachelor's degree in vocal music and her master's degree in vocal music education, the latter in 1977. Later, she earned her doctorate in music and education from Columbia University's Teacher's College in 1992.

Cooper established herself as a pianist and vocalist in the '70s and '80s in San Francisco, where she had a long tenure at the Hyatt Hotel on Union Square. She also freelanced with trumpeter Eddie Henderson and drummer Donald Bailey, and was in the house band at the Jazz Workshop, where she performed with saxophonists Eddie Harris, Red Holloway and David "Fathead" Newman and singer Jimmy Witherspoon, et al. After moving to New York, Cooper led a duo at the Renaissance Hotel, both singing and playing piano. She also worked as a solo singer/pianist at the Marriott Marquis Hotel and the Helmsley Palace Hotel. She has appeared in such clubs as the Blue Note and Birdland in Manhattan and Trumpets in Montclair, N.J., and as an accompanist, she backed singer Gloria Lynne at the Chicago Jazz Festival. In 2001, Cooper teamed with Henderson, drummer Yoron Israel and bassist Ron McClure for her new CD, "Day By Day."

Cooper's teaching career began in 1970 at Lebanon High School in Lebanon, Missouri. Later, from 1978-1988, she taught voice and piano and conducted the chamber choir at Chabot College in Hayward, California. In New York, Cooper supervised student music teachers at Columbia University's Teacher's College, where she also taught applied voice and piano. From 1992-1998, she taught at the Lee Strasberg Theatre Institute. Since 1989, she has been affiliated with Long Island University in Brooklyn, where she is currently an Assistant Professor of Music. Cooper instructs applied private voice, voice class, vocal jazz ensemble, piano class, music fundamentals, jazz keyboard harmony, and directs the LIU chorus.

The People Who Made The Music

The composers in **Sing JAZZ!** (listed in alphabetical order) range from some of the early giants of the music to some of its finest contemporary practitioners. Many of the lyricists are established greats while others are little-known but important members of the world jazz community. Their words are creative, thoughtful, vital, even provocative and humorous. These lyrics enhance the compositions, offering singers a wealth of new material with which to express themselves.

ROB BARGAD (b. 09/07/62)

Boston-native Bargad attended the jazz program at Rutgers University in New Jersey, then moved to New York in 1984. He played piano, first with singers Dakota Staton and Little Jimmy Scott, then vibes master Lionel Hampton (to whom he was recommended by a Rutgers professor, saxophonist Paul Jeffrey), the Harper Brothers and most notably, the late cornetist Nat Adderley. Bargad has also led his own bands since the late '80s.

A fine writer, his songs have been recorded by Adderley, saxophonist Vincent Herring and singer-pianist Dena DeRose; the latter recorded *Another World*, a tale of sadness and longing brought on by a dream of an ideal love that, of course, disappears upon waking.

PAMELA BASKIN-WATSON (b. 07/22/53)

Baskin-Watson is a classically trained pianist; in her professional life, she has specialized in composing songs and lyrics, and arranging for vocal ensembles. She studied at the University of Missouri and the University of Miami before relocating to New York, where she was music director of the Harlem School of the Arts' Vocal Jazz Ensemble. Baskin-Watson, who is married to alto saxophonist Bobby Watson, is also a member of New Renaissance, a vocal trio. Art Blakey, Kevin Mahogany, Betty Carter, the Boys Choir of Harlem and James Williams are among those who have recorded her songs, lyrics and arrangements.

In *The Love We Had Yesterday*, Baskin-Watson emotively reflects on a relationship that has ended, observing how the many things the couple once shared are now, sadly, just memories; what once were splendid possibilities are forever lost.

WALTER BOLDEN (b. 12/17/25, d. 02/07/02)

Drummer Bolden's name may not be that well known, but he played with the best in jazz for over 50 years until his death in 2002. Among the artists who have employed his firm, resilient kit work are Stan Getz, Horace Silver, Gigi Gryce, Gerry Mulligan, Sonny Rollins, Ray Bryant, George Shearing, Art Farmer and Annie Ross. In the late '70s, he recorded his only solo album. During that time, he also contributed tunes to the book of Art Taylor's Wailers, including *Mr. A.T. Revisited*.

With lyric by R. Rachel Mackin, that tune is titled *Do It Again*, and describes how the little things from someone special—a smile, a look, a few well chosen words—can make another emotionally soar.

RUBY BRAFF (b. 03/16/27)

Braff is a unique cornetist and trumpeter who cites Louis Armstrong as his main influence and inspiration. In a career that spans six decades, he has worked and/or recorded with many greats in traditional jazz, among them clarinetists Pee Wee Russell and Benny Goodman, pianists Ellis Larkins, Joe Sullivan and Roger Kellaway, trombonist Vic Dickenson and tenormen Scott Hamilton and Bud Freeman. He has also been heard with Tony Bennett.

Braff's brief *We're All Through* uses straight-forward, concise language to depict how musicians feel at the end of a gig.

CLIFFORD BROWN (b. 10/30/30; d. 06/27/56)

An influential trumpeter with dazzling technique, deep tunefulness and a bold, brassy tone, Brown was in the limelight for just five years (he died in a car accident at age 25) yet his mark on jazz is indelible. Early performances at jam sessions with Dizzy Gillespie, Charlie Parker and Fats Navarro (his major influences) led to work with R&B bandleader Chris Powell, Lionel Hampton and Tadd Dameron through 1953. Brown was then heard briefly with Art Blakey before teaming with Max Roach and forming their heralded quintet. His tunes *Joy Spring* and *Daahoud* are jazz classics.

Singer-pianist Meredith d'Ambrosio's words to the latter, included here as *Beloved*, describe, in contemporary language that suits Brown's driving jazz song to a tee, the about-to-burst thrill of love at first sight. Michael Stillman's lyric to *Joy Spring*, here called *When We're Alone*, explores in playful, upbeat terms the wonderful feeling of falling in love with one's beloved again and again.

DONALD BROWN (b. 03/28/54)

Pianist-composer Brown's career has been diverse. Though best known in jazz, he has also worked with such R&B and blues artists as Al Green, B.B. King and Ann Peebles. A graduate of Memphis State University, Brown's jazz associations have included Art Blakey, Freddie Hubbard, Wynton Marsalis, Bobby Hutcherson, Woody Shaw, trumpeter Eddie Henderson, saxophonist Kenny Garrett and many more; he has also been a leader, and has released numerous CDs. A vibrant writer, his tunes, such as *Episode From A Village Dance* and *Smile Of The Snake*, have been recorded by Blakey, James Williams, saxophonists Ralph Moore and James Spaulding and trumpeter Bill Mobley. Long active in education, Brown has been associate professor of music at the University of Tennessee at Knoxville since 1988.

The composer's *I Love It When You Dance That Way*, with lyrics by he and his wife, the classical pianist Dorothy

Brown, explores the wealth of pleasures that can come from dancing with a potential lover.

OSCAR BROWN, JR. (b. 10/10/26)

Early in his career, singer-composer Brown wrote songs recorded by Mahalia Jackson and Max Roach (the latter as part of the "We Insist! Freedom Now Suite"), but it was the 1960 Columbia album "Sin 'n' Soul" that thrust him into the jazz limelight. An actor and a performer, Brown wrote the stage show "Kicks And Company" and appeared in other shows. He has written numerous vocalese lyrics to classic tunes such as Horace Silver's *Doodlin'*.

Brown's *Honeydo* lightly describes the woes of a hen-pecked husband who, yearning for a moment's rest, is nonetheless forever doing his wife's bidding.

RAY BRYANT (b. 12/24/31)

A pianist versatile in swing, blues and bebop styles, Bryant has had a long and very successful career. Following performances in his native Philadelphia with guitarist Tiny Grimes, he was house pianist at the Blue Note club with Charlie Parker, Lester Young, Miles Davis, et al. Bryant moved to New York in the mid-'50s. There, he was heard with Carmen McRae, Sonny Rollins, Dizzy Gillespie and Curtis Fuller before becoming a leader. He has made numerous recordings for Columbia, Prestige, Cadet and Pablo Records. His song *Little Susie* was a hit in the '50s, his version of *The Madison Time* reached #30 on the Billboard charts in 1960, and his *Cubano Chant* has been recorded by many artists.

One Fine Day, the vocal version of the latter outfitted with zesty words by L. Aziza Miller, tells of the joy of merging with a new love, one who makes all past sadness disappear, who makes the passing days and nights glow with magic.

Meant To Be!, a vocal treatment of Bryant's *Chicken 'An Dumplings*, has a lyric by the noted Dutch singer Fleurine, who has penned words to tunes by Kenny Dorham, Thad Jones and Tom Harrell. Here, the narrator describes how the wind, the stars and the birds all tell her to love one special man; unfortunately, he's not listening.

JON BURR (b. 05/22/53)

Bassist-composer Burr has also played piano, clarinet and bassoon. He studied at the University of Illinois, then moved to New York in 1975. He has played with Buddy Rich, Lee Konitz, Gerry Mulligan, Tony Bennett, Chet Baker, pianist Roland Hanna and others, and has led a quintet. He has also performed with classical ensembles. His songs have been performed and/or recorded by Baker and the Mel Lewis Jazz Orchestra.

Burr's *Sea Breeze* describes in well-chosen words and phrases the remarkable feelings that arise from being by the ocean on a gorgeous day with the one you love.

SARA CASSEY (b. 04/01/29; d. 05/05/66)

Cassey was a Detroit native; among her associates as a youth was pianist Barry Harris. A pianist who apparently never performed publicly, she worked in the offices of Riverside Records in New York in the mid-to-late '50s. Cassey wrote several pieces which were recorded, including *Very Near Blue* (Clark Terry), *Windflower* (guitarist Herb Ellis), and *Warm Blue Stream* (pianist Hank Jones and singer Jean Turner). Dotty Wayne's lyric to the latter employs images of wingless flight and flowing water to depict the thrill of being swept away by love's embrace.

PAUL CHAMBERS (b. 04/22/35; d. 01/04/69)

A superb bassist, Chambers was top-notch in every department: tone, timekeeping, note choice and soloing; his arco improvisations are state of the art. He played and/or recorded with most of the greats from the mid-'50s to the mid-'60s, including Miles Davis (1955–63), Sonny Rollins, Sonny Stitt and J.J. Johnson. He appeared on many fine Prestige albums with pianist Red Garland and Art Taylor and was a member of pianist Wynton Kelly's trio, with drummer Jimmy Cobb.

Chambers recorded a handful of albums as a leader, one of which produced his oft-recorded blues, *Whims of Chambers*, to which R. Rachel Mackin has written words and which is called *Chillin'*. The lyric speaks of a lover emphatically informing his or her friends that since it's Friday night, the evening will be spent laying back and grooving with that significant other, "chillin'" to be precise, and that three is most definitely a crowd.

MICHAEL COCHRANE (b. 09/04/48)

A forward-leaning yet strongly swinging modern pianist, Cochrane studied with the noted Boston-based piano teacher Madame Margaret Chaloff (mother of baritone saxophonist Serge Chaloff) and the inimitable Jaki Byard. In a fruitful career, he has performed and/or recorded with saxophonists Michael Brecker, Sonny Fortune and Chico Freeman and trumpeters Clark Terry, Valery Ponomarev and Jack Walrath. He has led a quintet that included Tom Harrell and saxophonist Bob Malach, and he has recorded several albums as a leader, including 1997's "Cutting Edge." He has also been a jazz educator at New York University, Rutgers University-Newark and Princeton University.

Two Reflect As One is the vocal rendition of Cochrane's *Waltz No. 1*. Here, charming words by Cheryl Pyle depict a variety of compelling images as a loving couple dances under the night sky.

Al COHN (b. 11/24/25; d. 02/15/88)

Dubbed "Mr. Music" for his prodigious talents as a tenor saxophonist, composer, arranger and orchestrator, Cohn from the mid-'40s through the late '50s performed with, and wrote for, the big bands of Boyd Raeburn, Woody Herman, Buddy Rich and Elliot Lawrence. Though he often appeared and recorded as a leader, his main association was with fellow tenorman Zoot Sims. Cohn also worked regularly on Broadway, orchestrating such shows as "Music, Music, Music" and "Sophisticated Ladies." Dave Frishberg's superb lyric to Cohn's tender *The Underdog* describes the joys and sorrows of putting your money, or your heart, on the one least likely to win. But then, as the song says, favorites don't always win.

MEREDITH D'AMBROSIO (b. 03/20/41)

Singer-pianist-composer d'Ambrosio is an artist whose original songs, and lyrics to those by others, always have a deep ring of truth. Her voice is not dynamic but she has a great rhythmic feel and she invests her fluid interpretations with a resounding tunefulness. Classical and jazz studies in the late-'40s-early-'50s made her a resourceful pianist. A leader since the mid-'50s, she often accompanies herself. When not, her sidemen are first-rate: trumpeters Tom Harrell and Randy Sandke, bassists Michael Moore and Major Holley, drummers Jake Hanna and Terry Clarke and pianists Bob Dorough and Eddie Higgins, who is her husband. She has released numerous fine albums on the Sunnyside label.

Meredith d'Ambrosio's *Why Do I Still Dream Of You?* explores how a particular lover has been unable over time to let go of one who has moved on, encountering that lover in dreams and thoughts, always seeking a fresh start. The composer's *Without Reason, Without Rhyme* also addresses a lost love that is not forgotten, an unrequited love that was perhaps heedlessly entered into and one that would gladly be entered into again, acknowledging the pain while embracing the pleasure.

TADD DAMERON (b. 02/21/17; d. 03/08/65)

A giant of bebop, Dameron had a wonderful melodic and harmonic imagination which he brought to compositions and arrangements for both small and big bands. Writing first for Harlan Leonard, Jimmie Lunceford and Billy Eckstine, Dameron in the late '40s composed and arranged for Dizzy Gillespie's big band. He also led and recorded with his own superb sextet that often featured trumpet great Fats Navarro. In the '50s and '60s, the man famed for such numbers as *Hot House*, *If You Could See Me Now* and *Our Delight* wrote compelling songs and arrangements for John Coltrane, Sonny Stitt, trumpeter Blue Mitchell and many others.

Dameron's *Never Been In Love*, with a dramatic lyric by Irving Reid, tells a timeless tale, that of a man whose heart has never been touched by anyone until now—and, oh, how glad he is that it's happened.

The ace English jazz singer Georgie Fame penned the words to *There's No More Blue Time*, the vocal version of Dameron's *A Blue Time*. Fame, in his typical upbeat, colloquial manner, depicts a fellow in very bad straits after his lover has gone her separate way, but who happily sings a different tune when a new love arrives.

WALTER DAVIS, JR. (b. 09/02/32; d. 06/02/90)

Bud Powell-influenced pianist Davis, who boasts a rich blues feeling, became a professional as a late teenager. He traveled with vocalist Babs Gonzales, then appeared in New York with Charlie Parker, Max Roach and Dizzy Gillespie through 1956. He later worked as a leader (he recorded the fine "Davis Cup" album for Blue Note), and with alto saxophonist Jackie McLean (who recorded his tune, *Greasy*), Donald Byrd, Sonny Rollins and Art Blakey, who recorded such Davis originals as *Uranus*, *Jodi* and *Gypsy Folk Tales*.

The pianist-lyricist's *A Being Such As You* describes a person's sense that they have encountered a new lover in a dream or even a past life, and explores the excitement and even intrigue that's developing now that the pair are embarked on a romance.

KENNY DORHAM (b. 08/30/24; d. 12/05/72)

Another modern jazz great, McKinley "Kenny" Dorham made one of the first influential bebop recordings in 1946 as part of the Be-Bop Boys with Bud Powell, Fats Navarro and Sonny Stitt, then went on to play with Charlie Parker. Dubbed "The Uncrowned King" for his lack of wide-spread recognition, Dorham, who had a lovely, warm tone and a deep melodic and harmonic ingenuity, made numerous remarkable recordings in the '50s and '60s, including those with Art Blakey's Jazz Messengers, pianist Horace Silver's quintet and Sonny Rollins, and as a leader for Riverside, New Jazz and Blue Note. As gifted a composer as he was an improviser, Dorham wrote such time-tested numbers as *Fair Weather*, *La Villa*, *Blue Bossa*, *Una Mas* and *Lotus Blossom*.

The trumpeter added his own lyric to *Fair Weather*. In words both simple and elegant, the song speaks of the peace and beauty that can be found in life when people embrace each other's basic humanity and spirit; indeed, then it would always be fair weather.

Rhyme Of Spring is based on Dorham's instrumental *Poetic Spring*. Lyricist Meredith d'Ambrosio works off that latter title in feeling, describing in tuneful language the possibilities for love to bloom, or perhaps to fade, in spring.

GEORGE DUVIVIER (b. 08/17/20; d. 07/11/85)

Known primarily as a bassist, Duvivier was one of the top accompanists of the late swing and bebop eras, backing Coleman Hawkins, Bud Powell, and so many more. Later, he was steadily active in the New York recording studios, working behind Frank Sinatra, Benny Goodman and multi-reed and woodwind artist Eric Dolphy, to name only three. Duvivier was also a college-educated composer and arranger who wrote for Jimmie Lunceford, Sy Oliver and others.

In Duvivier's *Alone With Just My Dreams*, the narrator describes in often-poetic terms the emptiness that is felt when a love affair is over.

CURTIS FULLER (b. 12/15/34)
After J.J. Johnson, Fuller is probably the most influential of modern trombonists. Born in Detroit, he played in that area with saxophonists Pepper Adams and Yusef Lateef and guitarist Kenny Burrell, then moved to New York in 1957. There, he played and/or recorded with Miles Davis, Gil Evans, John Coltrane (on the famed "Blue Train" session for Blue Note), Bud Powell, the Jazztet, Quincy Jones and Sonny Clark. Later, Fuller performed in Art Blakey's Jazz Messengers (1961–65) and was a sideman with Count Basie, Benny Golson, and Blakey again (1977–78). He recorded widely as a leader and is a founding member of the Timeless All-Stars with Cedar Walton, Bobby Hutcherson, et al.
Fuller's *One Dream Gone*, instrumentally known as *The Court*, has a lyric by Fleurine that tells of an undaunted woman, sure of her own worth, quietly reflecting on the end of a love affair and certain that she will love again. *Sweet And True*, the vocal version of Fuller's *Sweetness*, has a delightful lyric by Catherine Whitney which suggests that love has a mind of its own, appreciating more someone who patiently awaits its sudden and joyous arrival than one who tirelessly seeks it out.

MATTHEW GEE (b. 11/25/25; d. 07/18/79)
A solid trombonist who worked with many jazz greats, Gee had a big tone and winning improvisational way. After playing with Coleman Hawkins and Dizzy Gillespie in the mid-'40s, he joined the bop-based band led by tenormen Sonny Stitt and Gene Ammons, then later played with Count Basie and Illinois Jacquet. He was on an important mid-'50s date by alto saxophonist Lou Donaldson for Blue Note that featured Kenny Dorham and Elmo Hope. He later rejoined Gillespie's big band, and, for a time, played with Duke Ellington. Gee made a first-rate album on Riverside that included his composition, *Gee*; he later wrote *Oh! Gee!* which has been recorded by many jazz artists. In the hip language of the '50s, it's a story about a fellow who hasn't the faintest idea why his "pretty baby" has gone, gone, gone, leaving him miserably on his own.

RODGERS GRANT (b. 01/18/36)
Best known as the pianist with Mongo Santamaria from 1962-69, Grant has written such tunes as *Yeh-Yeh* (co-composed with Pat Patrick), *Morning Star* and *Dealer Takes Four*. Among those who have recorded his works are Santamaria, Lambert, Hendricks & Bavan, saxophonists Stan Getz, Ralph Moore and Sonny Fortune and drummer T.S. Monk.
Grant's *The Gift Of Love* imaginatively describes how a woman's freely given love can open the heart of a receptive though perhaps slightly apprehensive man, enabling him to love in return.
In the pianist's *One Heart's Dream*, Catherine Whitney's lyric speaks of the power of love and of its intransigence, how even between two who love each other, it may waver but belief can make it whole again.

WARDELL GRAY (b. 02/13/21; d. 05/25/55)
A masterful tenor saxophonist who mixed the supple fluidity of tenor innovator Lester Young with the melodic breakthroughs of altoist Charlie Parker, Gray personified the transition from swing to bebop. He was heard with many greats, from Count Basie and Benny Goodman to Tadd Dameron and Dexter Gordon (with whom he recorded the timeless two-tenor battle, *The Chase)*. His solo on his own blues, *Twisted*, became a classic when Annie Ross penned words to it and recorded it in 1952. Her lyrics, employing an ear-pleasing, humorous attitude, colorfully depict a very bright, happy soul who is more than just a little bit wacky.

AL GREY (b. 06/06/25; d. 03/24/00)
A trombonist with a flair for swinging solos on both open horn and with the plunger mute, Al Grey played with bandleaders Benny Carter, Jimmie Lunceford, Lucky Millinder and Lionel Hampton (1948–52); his muted work was first spotlighted with the latter. He later worked with Arnett Cobb, Oscar Pettiford and Count Basie (1957–61, 1964-70). He also co-led sextets with several tenormen, including Billy Mitchell and Buddy Tate. This spirited artist remained active until shortly before his death.
Grey's *Al's Mist* has been outfitted with a lyric by Meredith d'Ambrosio and is vocally known as *Love Is Forever*. Here, in delicate words, she tells of the transitory nature of all things, advising the listener that if there is love in one's life, nurture it, embrace it, treasure it, for who knows what tomorrow will bring.

JOHNNY GRIFFIN (b. 04/24/28)
A tenor saxophonist of amazing energy and invention, Griffin was influenced by such revered artists as Johnny Hodges, Charlie Parker and Ben Webster. He was first heard prominently with Lionel Hampton's orchestra from 1945–47. A decade later, he was one of the preeminent artists on his instrument. His solo albums in the mid-to-late '50s demonstrated he was an improvisational master; so did tenures and recordings with Art Blakey, Thelonious Monk and the two-tenor band he co-led with Eddie "Lockjaw" Davis. For the past four decades he has lived in Europe, where he has played with Bud Powell, the Kenny Clarke-Francy Boland big band and Dizzy Gillespie. Mostly he has been a leader, and he regularly returns to the U.S. to perform. Among his better-known tunes are *The JAMFs Are Coming, Chicago Calling* and *Soft And Furry*.
For the latter, Eddie Jefferson, the inventor of vocalese and one of the greatest jazz singers ever, wrote a love-conquers-all lyric offering the point of view that the wealth found in true love essentially makes one's problems either solvable or simply irrelevant.

GIGI GRYCE (b. 11/28/25; d. 03/17/83)
Gryce was an alto saxophonist who had a strong influence as a composer and arranger. He studied at the Boston Conservatory and on a Fulbright scholarship with composers Nadia Boulanger and Arthur Honegger in Paris in 1952. He performed and/or recorded with many of the giants, among them Max Roach, Clifford Brown, Tadd Dameron, Thelonious Monk and Art Farmer, and was active as co-leader of The Jazz Lab with Donald Byrd in the late '50s. His tunes *Minority* and *Nica's Tempo* have become jazz standards.
Gryce's *You'll Always Be The One I Love* expresses the joy that comes from being head-over-heels in love.

FLETCHER HENDERSON (b. 12/18/1898; d. 12/29/52)
A core figure in swing music, Henderson began leading a large ensemble in the mid '20s; among his sidemen were such innovators as trumpeter Louis Armstrong and saxophonist Coleman Hawkins. In the mid-to-late '30s, Henderson wrote hard-driving arrangements for Benny Goodman that were essential to the clarinetist's popularity. Henderson's appealing blues, *Soft Winds*, has been recorded by many modern jazz musicians, including Art Blakey, and it was a hit for singer Dinah Washington in 1954. In that song, lyricist Fred Royal tells of a lonely woman entreating the winds to gently urge her lover, who is far away in both mind and body, to please come back home.

EDDIE HIGGINS (b. 02/21/32)
Higgins is a solid pianist in the mainstream tradition. Born in Cambridge, Massachusetts, he made his name in Chicago where he led trios at the famed London House from 1957–69, and where he recorded with Lee Morgan and Wayne Shorter and as a leader. He then moved to Ft. Lauderdale, Fla. (he also has a home on Cape Cod), working with saxophonist/trumpeter Ira Sullivan, and at jazz parties and on jazz cruises. In 1988, he married singer-pianist Meredith d'Ambrosio, whom he often accompanies. His recent albums are on the Sunnyside label.
Higgins' *Just A Dream*, which he instrumentally called *Falando De Orlando*, has a lyric by d'Ambrosio that, with well-crafted images, deftly describes a late night romantic encounter.

LONNIE HILLYER (b. 03/25/40; d. 07/01/85)
A Detroit native, Hillyer was a teenaged friend of alto saxophonist Charles McPherson; they both studied with bebop maestro Barry Harris. Hillyer played with Yusef Lateef and Joe Henderson before moving to New York in 1961, where he worked and recorded with Harris, Charles Mingus and McPherson, all into the '70s. He also co-led a group with saxophonist Charles Davis. He was a fearless soloist armed with a crackling tone and keen melodic invention.
Hillyer's *Tomorrow* concerns a person who has loved and lost but who isn't about to sit around and mope because

tomorrow is another day, and who knows what fortune has in store.

BERTHA HOPE (b. 11/08/36)
The wife of pianist Elmo Hope, Bertha Hope is also a beguiling bebop-based pianist. Initially classically trained, Hope took jazz piano lessons from Richie Powell, Bud Powell's brother. She played in Los Angeles in the late-'50s with Johnny Otis and also led a trio. She and her husband moved to New York in 1961, where she both studied and performed. Her solo album debut, "In Search of Hope," with drummer Billy Higgins and bassist Walter Booker, was released in 1990. Her latest, "Nothin' But Love," came out in 2000.
Hope's *You Know Who!* offers powerful advice: when you're alone and life is giving you a rough go, just sit tight, be calm and take it easy on the one person that can always be counted on: that's right—you.

ELMO HOPE (b. 06/27/23; d. 05/19/67)
A disciple of bop legends Bud Powell and Thelonious Monk, Hope was one of those superb artists who never managed to gain proper recognition for his gifts. He was active in New York during the early-to-mid '50s, playing and recording with Clifford Brown and Sonny Rollins, and then in California, where he played with tenorist Harold Land and his own trio. He returned to New York in 1961, recording there as a leader with such stellar sidemen as John Coltrane, Hank Mobley, Jimmy Heath, Donald Byrd, Paul Chambers and Philly Joe Jones. Hope's music lives on, judging by the number of young musicians who record his tunes—and by a recent tribute concert in New York in October 2001.
The vocal version of Hope's *Chips* is called *Just A Little Dreamer*. R. Rachel Mackin's lyric lines flow smoothly from one to the next, telling about a person whose love is unrequited but who remains undaunted because there's always the chance that things just might work out.

SHEILA JORDAN (b. 11/18/28)
A decidedly creative and persuasive jazz vocalist, Jordan in the early '50s studied the music of Charlie Parker and wrote words to his tunes. The bop-oriented Jordan later began to investigate free jazz. Married to bop pianist Duke Jordan from 1952–62, Jordan has also performed with Lee Konitz, trombonist Roswell Rudd, pianist Steve Kuhn and in a duo setting with bassist Harvie Swartz. An acclaimed songwriter, she has recorded numerous albums including the recent "From the Heart" and "The Very Thought of You."
Jordan's *Ballad For Miles* evokes the magic of listening to Miles Davis.

JONNY KING (b. 02/02/65)
An energetic, modern pianist whose enterprising work bears the influence of Herbie Hancock and McCoy Tyner, King studied with Tony Aless (who played with Woody Herman, Charlie Parker and Stan Getz) and Mulgrew

Miller. Leading his own bands since he was 17, King has also appeared with Out of the Blue, and saxophonists Joshua Redman and Eddie Harris. A practicing copyright attorney, he has released several fine CDs; saxophonist Billy Pierce and drummers Billy Drummond and Tony Reedus, among others, have recorded his tunes. *Heavenly!*, which is King's instrumental *Tryst*, has a lyric by R. Rachel Mackin that playfully and spiritedly describes the idea that a prized partner has been sent in some magical, otherworldly fashion.

HAROLD LAND (b. 02/18/28; d. 07/27/2001)

Tenor saxophonist Land, who played supple lines with a muscular tone, gained renown as a key member of the Clifford Brown-Max Roach quintet, a band he left in 1956 to return to Los Angeles (he was originally from Houston, TX.) There, he worked and recorded as a sideman with bassist Curtis Counce and bandleader Gerald Wilson, co-led superb groups with bassist Red Mitchell, Blue Mitchell and Bobby Hutcherson and occasionally appeared as a soloist with Tony Bennett. He was also a member of the Timeless All-Stars.
Land's *Rapture* is vocally known as *That Magic Rapture*; Meredith d'Ambrosio's lyric expresses the depth of joy that can come from love at first sight.

MELBA LISTON (b. 01/13/26; d. 04/23/99)

Liston was, like Mary Lou Williams before her, one of the very few female musicians to be fully accepted into the male-dominated jazz milieu. Equally impressive as a trombonist, composer and arranger, she was heard with the bands of Gerald Wilson and Count Basie in the mid-to-late '40s, then in the '50s intermittently with the big band of Dizzy Gillespie and Quincy Jones. She was then known mainly as a writer for Basie, Duke Ellington, pianist Randy Weston, and as a staff arranger at Motown Records. When a stroke took away her ability to play in 1985, she learned to write music on a computer.
Liston's *We Never Kissed (What A Shame)* describes the sorrow that arises when that lover that might have been ends up with another.

CURTIS LUNDY (b. 01/10/55)

A resourceful bassist and composer, Lundy has worked with such top-drawer artists as Betty Carter, Art Blakey, Freddie Hubbard, saxophonist Pharoah Sanders and pianist John Hicks. He has also served as director of the ARC gospel Choir. His two albums, "Just be Yourself" and "Against All Odds," are worth seeking out. Lundy, the brother of singer Carmen Lundy, has written provocative tunes recorded by Hicks, Bobby Watson and others.
Singer Kurt Elling recently recorded Lundy's ballad, *Orange Blossom*, as *Orange Blossoms In Summertime*. Here, Elling lyrically employs the sweet smell of orange blossoms to recall the depth of attachment to one's beloved when the pair are far apart.

RONNIE MATHEWS (b. 12/02/35)

A pianist originally influenced by Bud Powell and Thelonious Monk, and later, to some degree, Herbie Hancock and McCoy Tyner, Mathews is capable of dynamic, moving performances. Since the early-'60s, he has been heard with many of the best in modern music, including Kenny Dorham, Max Roach, Art Blakey, Roy Haynes, Johnny Griffin, Clifford Jordan and a group co-led by drummer Louis Hayes and Woody Shaw. In the '90s, he was heard in drummer T.S. Monk's sextet that also featured trumpeter Don Sickler and saxophonist Bobby Porcelli.
Mathews' *The Man With The Magic*, instrumentally known as *Dorian*, has a lyric by the wondrous jazz singer Abbey Lincoln. Lincoln's narrator describes the potent allure of a special man, a man of mischief and surprise who can dazzle with a look, thrill with a word. Happily, she's talking about her man.

TOM McINTOSH (b. 02/06/27)

McIntosh's fine trombone playing has been overshadowed by his excellence as a composer. A graduate of the Juilliard School, he first came to renown as a member of James Moody's band, and then with the Jazztet; he also played with and wrote for the Thad Jones-Mel Lewis Jazz Orchestra and recorded with Lionel Hampton, Hubert Laws and Milt Jackson. In 1969, McIntosh moved to California to concentrate on film and TV writing; his soundtracks include "Shaft's Big Score" and "Slither." His tunes *Cup Bearers* and *With Malice Toward None* have been recorded by numerous jazz musicians.
The vocal version of *Cup Bearers* is called *Cup Of Life*, with words by Meredith d'Ambrosio. The lyric poetically describes a suitor's entreaty to a prospective mate, employing a variety of images to convey the power and magic that can be found in a cup filled with love.

SERGIO MIHANOVICH (b. 05/08/37)

In his career, Buenos Aires native Mihanovich has been active in many areas: writing soundtracks for Argentine films and theatrical productions; working in nightclubs; recording in both jazz (he has performed and recorded with saxophonist Gato Barbieri) and pop settings; as an educator; and as a writer of both music and words.
His best-known work is *Sometime Ago*, which has been recorded by Cannonball Adderley, Stan Getz, George Shearing, singer Irene Kral and others. This lilting waltz describes from the vantage point of time past how love danced delightfully into two lives and then, sadly, made its departure.
In *Love And Deception*, the narrator advises men who have been involved in an unrequited love affair to be a bit thick-skinned the next time because, he says, in love honesty and directness may not always be the best policy.

HANK MOBLEY (b. 07/07/30; d. 05/30/86)

Like his colleague Kenny Dorham, tenor saxophonist Hank Mobley was a superb musician who, despite profound musical knowledge, a great ear for melody and a mellow tone, was mostly overlooked by both critics and the public. But musicians loved him. Horace Silver, for one, called him his "hippest" tenor soloist. Early appearances and recordings with Max Roach and Dizzy Gillespie led to his teaming in 1954 with Dorham, Silver, bassist Doug Watkins and Art Blakey in the Jazz Messengers. He then played with Silver, Roach once again, Blakey and Miles Davis (1960–62), and later co-led a group with Cedar Walton. Mobley is revered for his numerous outstanding Blue Note recordings and such originals as *This I Dig of You*, *Funk In Deep Freeze* and *Bossa De Luxe*.

Bebe Herring's words to the latter, vocally known as *Garden In The Sand*, talk of a garden that continues to grow despite the harsh, arid environment of the Sahara desert. But there is another message as well: that whatever is loved deeply will thrive no matter the circumstances.

GRACHAN MONCUR III (b. 06/03/37)

A modern-minded improviser, composer and Juilliard School graduate, trombonist Moncur established himself in New York in the late '50s and '60s, appearing and/or recording with Ray Charles, the Jazztet, Sonny Rollins, Joe Henderson and in a quintet led by saxophonist Jackie McLean that featured Bobby Hutcherson and drummer Tony Williams. His first Blue Note album, "Evolution," drew critical acclaim. He later formed 360 Degree Music Experience with drummer Beaver Harris and played with organist Big John Patton, singer Cassandra Wilson and saxophonist Frank Lowe. He has also been active in music education.

The trombonist's *The Coaster* describes the feeling of love, be it on a real or metaphorical sloop at sea, sighting the stars above, or in a lover's arms, with warmth everywhere.

J.R. MONTEROSE (b. 01/19/27; d. 09/16/93)

A tenor saxophonist with a light though penetrating tone and a keen melodic and rhythmic approach, Monterose always brought something special to the bandstand or recording studio. He was active in New York City and upstate New York, on the West Coast and in Europe; his major sideman associations included Buddy Rich, Charles Mingus, Kenny Dorham (he recorded with the latter pair) and pianist George Wallington, but he was mostly a leader. Monterose's debut for Blue Note, featuring Horace Silver, is first-rate; so are "The Message" and "A Little Pleasure," both with piano ace Tommy Flanagan.

The saxophonist's *Alone Again* speaks of how, after a relationship has ended, the ensuing period of solitude and reflection can lead to a deeper understanding of the essential issues of life.

RALPH MOORE (b. 12/24/56)

One of the most vital and musical saxophonists of the modern era, London-born Moore attended the Berklee College of Music (1975–78) and has since played and recorded with the best: Horace Silver, Freddie Hubbard, Roy Haynes, Kenny Barron, Cedar Walton and J.J. Johnson. From 1995, he has appeared in guitarist Kevin Eubanks' NBC Tonight Show Orchestra. Employing a warm, luminescent tone and an agile improvisatory imagination, Moore has recorded several superior albums; he is also a composer of depth, feeling and excitement.

On *Don't Go*, the vocal version of Moore's *Josephine*, Meredith d'Ambrosio crafts a brief, tender portrait of a lover entreating another who might be somewhat shy and reserved into allowing deeper emotions and physical expressions to surface.

KIRK NUROCK (b. 02/28/48)

Nurock, a talented composer and pianist, is one of the many should-be-better-knowns of contemporary music. Son of a jazz pianist, Nurock studied at the Juilliard School and at the Eastman Arranging Laboratory, and has played with Dizzy Gillespie, Sonny Stitt, Phil Woods and Lee Konitz, and has written songs for singers Theo Bleckmann and Sheila Jordan. A book of his works, "The Music of Kirk Nurock, Vol. 1," was published in 1991. He is also active as an educator.

In *I'm Movin' On*, the ace singer Judy Niemack's lyric speaks of the never-easy process of letting go of the self-defeating interpersonal attachments, possessions and emotions that keep us mired, thus releasing ourselves and moving toward the freely-lived life.

On *A Something In A Summer's Day*, Nurock has adapted Emily Dickinson's poem, "XII: Psalm Of The Day." The lyric speaks of the subtle glories possessed by each part of the day and asks that we simply feel and trust the splendor of these moments. If we look to them for more than they can offer, their magic will disappear.

JOHN ODDO (b. 03/21/53)

Oddo, a top-drawer pianist, composer and arranger, graduated from the Eastman School and subsequently, from the early-to-mid-'80s, played and arranged for Woody Herman. Later, he served as singer Rosemary Clooney's pianist, arranger and conductor.

Oddo's *Especially For You . . .* is included here as *All My Love, Especially For You*. Pamela Baskin-Watson's words speak of a person who, after dissolving a relationship due to the fear and doubt that accompanied potential commitment, reflects on all the good things that the relationship had and feels the courage to try again, if only the former lover would be willing.

FRITZ PAUER (b. 10/14/43)

An acclaimed European pianist and composer, Pauer has been active since the early '60s, and has played and/or recorded with such notables as Art Farmer and Benny

Bailey. His compositions have found favor with many jazz artists; Farmer and singer Vanessa Rubin, for example, have recorded *Fairytale Countryside*.

That number, with words by Pauer and Rubin, is titled *Like An Old Song*. It describes the wonderful feelings, so familiar yet sometimes seeming to come from afar, that can be found by looking inside yourself and just listening to your thoughts.

The acclaimed bebop-based vocalist Mark Murphy added a lyric to Pauer's *Sound Within An Empty Room*. Included here as simply *Empty Room*, the song tellingly laments the apparent dissolution of a love affair and the hope that a new romance will soon take its place.

CECIL PAYNE (b. 12/14/22)

Initially an alto saxophonist who switched to baritone saxophone, Payne was the major artist on that larger horn during the bebop period. Deeply influenced by Charlie Parker, he played and/or recorded in big bands led by Dizzy Gillespie, saxophonist James Moody, Tadd Dameron, Count Basie, Woody Herman and Illinois Jacquet, and small groups fronted by Kenny Dorham, John Coltrane, Gigi Gryce and trombonist Jimmy Cleveland. He has also been a member of the Dameron tribute band, Dameronia. Active into the new century, Payne has also been a leader, making numerous first-rate sides for Savoy, Signal and Muse.

Payne's *Full Moonlight*, instrumentally known as *Full Moonlight And Stars Made Of Silver*, includes words by Rob Bargad that describe the happiness one feels being with a cherished partner outdoors under a full moon.

BOBBY PORCELLI (b. 12/16/37)

Alto saxophonist Porcelli is an exciting, vital-toned New York-based player comfortable in a variety of mediums. In the Latin realm, he has played with Tito Rodriguez, Machito, Tito Puente and Mongo Santamaria (intermittently between 1967–1991). His associations in the modern jazz milieu include the Kenny Dorham-Joe Henderson big band, bassist Chuck Israels and T.S. Monk—as a founding member of the drummer's sextet. *It's All In The Mind*, the vocal version of Porcelli's *Rejuvenate*, includes lyrics by Fleurine. Here, using upbeat, dynamic language, she prods an unspecified protagonist to let the winds of change blow through mind and being and to start living a new, rejuvenated life—now!

JULIAN PRIESTER (b. 6/29/35)

Priester has brought a vital, spirited style of trombone playing to a wealth of artists. In his native Chicago, he played with bluesmen Muddy Waters and Bo Diddley, forward-looking bandleader Sun Ra, the master swing era vibist Lionel Hampton and blues-jazz singing marvel Dinah Washington. Locating in New York in the late '50s, Priester was heard with Max Roach's sextet alongside Eric Dolphy and Clifford Jordan, then later Art Blakey's Jazz Messengers, McCoy Tyner, Donald Byrd and Slide Hampton. In the '70s, he was part of Duke Ellington's

orchestra and Herbie Hancock's sextet and also played with pianists Stanley Cowell and Red Garland. The trombonist has lived in Seattle since the '80s, during which time he has toured with bassist Dave Holland. He is currently on faculty at the Cornish College of the Arts.

FREDDIE REDD (b. 05/29/28)

Redd, a subtle bebop-based pianist with an ear for the blues, was acclaimed for his score for the off-Broadway play, "The Connection," in which he appeared in New York and in Europe from 1959–1963. Intermittently active in Manhattan, San Francisco and Los Angeles, Redd has often worked as a leader but has also been a sideman with Oscar Pettiford, Art Blakey, Art Farmer and Gigi Gryce and trumpeter Rolf Ericson. He recently released an album of new material on his own label.

Redd's *Merry Christmas* has words by Van Dee Sickler, father of Don Sickler. Vocally known as *Christmas Morning In The Snow*, the song gracefully heralds that special holiday, depicting the splendor when there is freshly fallen snow and time shared with loved ones to brighten the day.

RENEE ROSNES (b. 03/24/62)

A masterful pianist and composer who has been hailed by her colleagues but has yet to receive deserved mainstream popularity, Rosnes is from Regina, Saskatchewan. She studied classical piano in both Vancouver and Toronto, and played with saxophonists Dave Liebman and Joe Farrell, among others. Moving to New York in 1986, she has appeared with Wayne Shorter, J.J. Johnson, Joe Henderson, Jon Faddis, the Carnegie Hall Jazz Band and James Moody. She has also led her own bands, which sometimes feature her husband, drummer Billy Drummond. Rosnes' multiple talents as composer, pianist and leader are heard on such first-rate albums as "As We Are Now," "Ancestors" and "With a Little Help from My Friends."

Rosnes' *For The Moment* is vocally known as *In The Moment*. Here, Shelley Brown, lyricist and flutist with the National Ballet Orchestra of Canada, uses a series of brief, well-drawn metaphors to compellingly describe the loneliness that follows love's departure.

In *Without You*, the vocal version of Rosnes' instrumental, *Malaga Moon*, Brown again employs images of stars and skies to lyrically describe the rapture a person feels being in love.

CHARLIE ROUSE (b. 04/06/24; d. 11/30/88)

An important sideman during the bebop years, tenor saxophonist Rouse was heard in the '40s and '50s with Dizzy Gillespie, Billy Eckstine, Tadd Dameron, Fats Navarro, Duke Ellington, Clifford Brown and with his own band, The Jazz Modes (co-led with French horn player Julius Watkins). Later, the man who played limber lines with a distinctive sound was best known for his lengthy tenure (1959-70) with Thelonious Monk. Rouse remained active post-Monk, particularly as one of the founding members of the cooperative group Sphere, dedicated initially to Monk's music.

My Little Sherri, the vocal version of Rouse's *Little Sherri*, has perky lyrics by Ben Sidran that tell of a young lad or lass who feels the glamorous pull of Hollywood and its environs. Still, as hip as all that might be, it's nothing compared to being with that special someone.

MILTON SEALEY (b. 06/02/28; d. 10/26/2000)
A Canadian pianist and composer, Sealey performed for many years at the Windows On The World restaurant in the former World Trade Center. Among his sidemen there was the great Louis Hayes.

Sealey's *I'll Remember Love*, instrumentally known as *The Setting Sun*, has a lyric by Catherine Whitney that tells of a lover reflecting on the ending of what was thought to be a life-long relationship, knowing that that love will never be forgotten.

The pianist's *Blue Love* is vocally known as *Who's Been Loving You?* L. Aziza Miller's words tenderly explore the blue feelings and the probing questions that fill one's mind when a love relationship is clearly on the wane.

NORMAN SIMMONS (b. 10/06/29)
Pianist-arranger-composer Simmons worked in his native Chicago with many notables, among them Clifford Jordan and trumpeter Paul Bascomb as well as Charlie Parker and Dexter Gordon-the latter pair as house pianist at the noted Bee Hive club. Moving to New York in 1959, he accompanied such singers as Betty Carter, Carmen McRae, Dakota Staton, Anita O'Day and Joe Williams, and played with the Johnny Griffin-Eddie "Lockjaw" Davis quintet and others. He arranged for many artists, including Williams, McRae, Griffin and pianist Ramsey Lewis—who had a hit (#19 in Billboard, 1966) with Simmons' version of *Wade in the Water*. Singers Jimmy Scott and Melissa Walker and saxophonists Griffin, Red Holloway and Scott Hamilton have recorded his songs.

Simmons' *You Are Mine (A Lullaby Of Motherhood)* celebrates the miracle of pregnancy as an expectant mother rhapsodizes to the growing child inside, stating her boundless love.

LUCKY THOMPSON (b. 06/16/24)
A tenor saxophonist with a big, breathy tone, agile imagination and quicksilver technique, Thompson was another artist who took his originally swing-oriented style and moved smoothly into the bebop idiom. He made notable recordings and/or appearances with Count Basie, Charlie Parker and Dizzy Gillespie, Thelonious Monk and Oscar Pettiford in the '40s and Miles Davis (as part of the famed *Walkin'* date for Prestige) and Stan Kenton in the '50s. In the next two decades, Thompson made several excellent albums for Prestige and Groove Merchant, then retired from the jazz scene. His compositions such as *Prey-Loot* have long proved of interest to modern musicians.

Thompson's *You Never Miss The Water Till The Well Runs Dry* offers a straying lover this timeless advice: you may not miss your used-to-be now while you're having your fun, but you sure will when that new love fades.

BOBBY TIMMONS (b. 12/19/35; d. 03/01/74)
A bluesy pianist who was also persuasive in the bop mode, Timmons played with Kenny Dorham's Jazz Prophets, Sonny Stitt and trumpeter Maynard Ferguson before joining Art Blakey (1958-59), then Cannonball Adderley (1959-60). He spent most of the rest of his career as a leader. Blakey recorded Timmons' first big hit, the gospel-like blues *Moanin'*, to which Jon Hendricks wrote the now well-known lyric, that he later recorded with Lambert, Hendricks and Ross. Adderley recorded Timmons' second extremely popular tune, *'Dis Here*. Timmons also composed such memorable works as *Dat Dere* and *So Tired*.

Moanin' tells of a bereft soul—alone, tired, sad—who asks for spiritual help for his predicament.

TOMMY TURRENTINE (b. 04/22/28; d. 05/13/97)
While Tommy Turrentine, the elder trumpet-playing brother of tenor saxophonist Stanley Turrentine, never stood in the limelight as his sibling did, he was a marvelous musician and composer. After initially working with Benny Carter, saxophonist Earl Bostic and Count Basie, Turrentine performed and/or recorded with Max Roach, Horace Parlan, Sonny Clark, Jackie McLean, Lou Donaldson, Dexter Gordon and Big John Patton. Among his tunes those artists recorded were *As Long As You're Living*, *Rastus* and *Midnight Mambo*. His lone album as a leader was on Time Records.

Turrentine's *Glo's Theme* is, with L. Aziza Miller's lyric, known as *Big Brown Eyes*; it speaks of a budding romance between two people whose eyes, we ultimately find out in a nice bit of surprise, are the same color.

As Long As You're Living, which the trumpeter wrote with trombonist Julian Priester, has, as the vocal *Long As You're Living*, a powerhouse lyric by Oscar Brown, Jr. In impassioned yet straightforward words, Brown, while pointing out that the clock is indeed ticking, delineates his core philosophy: live now, not later, live with zeal and live with empathy for our fellow humans.

MAL WALDRON (b. 08/16/26)
Waldron, who employs a spare, thoughtful yet distinctly driving piano style, has had a fruitful career. Armed with a degree in composition from NYC's Queens College, the pianist played with tenor saxophonist Ike Quebec in the late '40s-early '50s, then with bassist Charles Mingus; he also distinguished himself as Billie Holiday's final accompanist, working with her from 1957-59. In the late '50s, he played on numerous albums on Prestige with such artists as Gene Ammons and John Coltrane, then recorded with Eric Dolphy and trumpeter Booker Little. Currently residing in Europe where he has appeared with

such artists as saxophonists Archie Shepp and Steve Lacy, Waldron is known for his classic ballad, *Soul Eyes*. Abbey Lincoln has written lyrics to Waldron's *Straight Ahead* that speak in crisp metaphors of the arduous road that life often presents and that to best navigate its pitfalls, one should act with care and judgment.

CEDAR WALTON (b. 01/17/34)

A majestic pianist, arranger, and composer in the modern idiom, Walton plays and writes with invention, swing and elegance. A native of Dallas who later moved to New York, he appeared with trombonist J.J. Johnson and the Jazztet before joining Art Blakey (1961–64), who recorded his now-jazz standard, *Mosaic*. Thereafter, he has been mainly a leader: co-leading a quartet with Clifford Jordan, fronting the quartet Eastern Rebellion as well as a trio. Walton has made scores of first-rate albums under his name, and as a sideman with Lee Morgan, Kenny Dorham, Freddie Hubbard, Abbey Lincoln, Milt Jackson and many others. He is also in demand as an arranger of dates for singers, among them Etta James, Ian Shaw and Freddie Cole. Other Walton compositions that are bedrocks of the modern jazz repertoire include *Ugetsu*, *Bolivia*, *Midnight Waltz* and *Mode for Joe*.
Mosaic is here called *Life's Mosaic*. The lyrics by John and Paula Hackett use vivid, inspiring language to celebrate diversity and illuminate the possibilities of each new day.

ROBERT "BOBBY" WATSON (b. 08/23/53)

The resourceful, vibrant alto saxophonist-composer Watson gained renown as Art Blakey's musical director (1977–81), contributing such tunes as *Time Will Tell* and *A Wheel Within a Wheel* to the book. He has since freelanced with Louis Hayes, Charli Persip, John Hicks and trumpeter Terumasa Hino. He has led his group, Horizon, since the early '80s, and is a founding member of the 29th Street Saxophone Quartet. An artist with many CDs under his name, Watson's other distinctive tunes such as *Appointment in Milano* have been recorded by Blakey, Hicks, James Williams, Wynton Marsalis, Kevin Mahogany, T.S. Monk and others. A graduate of the University of Miami, Watson is director of the jazz studies program at the University of Missouri in Kansas City.
The vocal version of *Appointment In Milano*, with a lyric by Watson's wife, Pamela Baskin-Watson, is called *Another Time, Another Place*. It tells of a man who has been estranged from his lover and hopes that when they meet again, they can return in mind, spirit and heart to the time when they were as one.
Watson and Baskin-Watson also collaborated on *Our Love Remains*, which speaks of how, through thick and thin, through closeness and periods spent apart, a man and a woman are enriched by their bond of love.

CHUCK WAYNE (b. 02/27/23; d. 07/29/97)

A principal swing-to-bop guitarist who delivered a glowing tone and smoothly contoured improvisatory lines, Wayne played in the mid-to-late '40s with such legends as Dizzy Gillespie, Bud Powell, Coleman Hawkins, Lester Young, George Shearing and Woody Herman. Later came performances and/or recordings with Zoot Sims, Gil Evans, Frank Sinatra, Sarah Vaughan, Duke Jordan, et al. Wayne was also an educator, teaching at the New England Conservatory of Music and the Mannes College of Music at the New School of Social Research. Wayne is the author of "The School of Chuck Wayne: Guitar Studies," three volumes detailing his unique approach to playing jazz guitar.
Wayne's *Baby, I'm Coming Home* is the tale of a wandering lover who realizes the wrong-headedness of his behavior and, with his partner's forgiveness, wants to make their relationship permanent, not transitory.

SCOTT WHITFIELD (b. 03/10/63)

Trombonist-composer-arranger-singer Whitfield started young: he has played trombone since he was nine and led his first band at age 14. He studied at Florida State University and The University of North Texas (formerly North Texas State). First active in Florida in a variety of settings, Whitfield then established himself in New York in the mid-'90s, playing with Nat Adderley, the Toshiko Akiyoshi Jazz Orchestra and as a leader of both instrumental ensembles and the Manhattan Vocal Project. The talented, straight-ahead artist's CDs include "To Be There" and the recently released "Hiding In Plain Sight."
When We Meet Again, the vocal version of Whifield's *Utopia*, has a lyric by singer Michael Andrew that describes how the strong feelings between two lovers will hold them close even though circumstances have forced them to be far apart.

JAMES WILLIAMS (b. 03/08/51)

A heartily swinging pianist and composer, Williams undertook early studies in his native Memphis, Tennessee, at the University of Memphis, then moved to Boston, where he taught at the Berklee College of Music (1974–77). He played with Art Blakey's Jazz Messengers (1977–81), during which time he introduced trumpeter Wynton Marsalis to Blakey, effectively starting the trumpeter's jazz career. Later, Williams freelanced with such top-drawer players as Sonny Stitt, Woody Shaw, Joe Henderson, Milt Jackson and Art Farmer; he has also regularly appeared and recorded as a leader. Long active in jazz education, Williams is the director of Jazz Studies at William Paterson University in Wayne, N.J. Such originals of his as *Ph.D.*, *Progress Report*, *Alter Ego* and *Old Times' Sake* have been widely recorded.
On the latter, vocally known as *For Old Times' Sake*, Pamela Baskin-Watson's words gracefully describe the myriad joys that can come from a long-term committed relationship.
You're My Alter Ego is the vocal version of *Alter Ego*. Here, Baskin-Watson's lyric celebrates the closeness and empathy that results when a new love holds the promise of lasting a lifetime.

Zan Stewart

A Selected Discography

Vocal and Instrumental Recordings

The vocal version title is listed first, with its recordings. If the vocal version hasn't been recorded, the instrumental title and its recordings follow immediately. If there is no indication of an instrumental recording, the title has not been recorded as an instrumental. The format is leader / title of album or CD (company and number [alternate release company and number]). Although not all of these recordings are in print, we have attempted to list currently-available release numbers.

ALL MY LOVE, ESPECIALLY FOR YOU - John Oddo & Pamela Baskin-Watson
instrumental: ESPECIALLY FOR YOU . . . - John Oddo
Woody Herman / Live At The Concord Jazz Festival (Concord 191)

ALONE AGAIN - J. R. Monterose
Carmelita Esposito / The Men I Love (Family Company 1)
instrumental: ALONE AGAIN - J. R. Monterose
Freddie Deronde / Spontaneous Effort (Igloo Productions 081)

ALONE WITH JUST MY DREAMS - George Duvivier
instrumental: ALONE WITH JUST MY DREAMS - George Duvivier
Joe Wilder / Alone With Just My Dreams (Musical Heritage Society 13348)
Rodney Whitaker / Ballads And Blues (Criss Cross 1167)

ANOTHER TIME, ANOTHER PLACE - Robert Watson & Pamela Baskin-Watson
Kevin Mahogany / Another Time, Another Place (Warner Bros 46699)
instrumental: APPOINTMENT IN MILANO - Robert Watson
T.S. Monk / Changing Of The Guard (Blue Note 89050)
Bobby Watson / Appointment In Milano (Red 123184)
Bobby Watson / Open Form Trio (Red 123231)
Bobby Watson / Post-Motown Bop (Blue Note 95148)

ANOTHER WORLD - Rob Bargad
Dena DeRose / Another World (Sharp Nine 1016)

BABY, I'M COMING HOME - Chuck Wayne
The Bebop Boys (sung by Kenny Hagood) (Savoy 2225)

BALLAD FOR MILES - Sheila Jordan
Sheila Jordan / Jazz Child (HighNote 7029)

A BEING SUCH AS YOU - Walter Davis, Jr.
instrumental: A BEING SUCH AS YOU - Walter Davis, Jr.
Walter Davis, Jr. / 400 Years Ago Tomorrow (Owl 020)
Walter Davis, Jr. / A Being Such As You (Red 123150)

BELOVED - Clifford Brown & Meredith d'Ambrosio
Meredith d'Ambrosio / Love Is For The Birds (Sunnyside 1101)
instrumental: DAAHOUD - Clifford Brown
Joe Albany & Warne Marsh / Right Combination (Milestone 6071 [OJC 1749])
Alan Broadbent / Away From You (Trend 558)
Alan Broadbent / Better Days (First Media Music 74004)
Clifford Brown / Jazz Immortal (Pacific Jazz LP 3 [Blue Note 32142])
Clifford Brown & Max Roach (Emarcy 26043 [Verve 543306])
Ray Bryant / Ray Bryant Trio (Prestige 7098 [OJC 793])
Frank Capp Quartet / Quality Time (Concord 4677)
Cecilia Coleman / Higher Standards (Interplay 9901)
Mad & Eddie Duran / From Here To The Moon (Milestone 9296)
Red Garland / Stepping Out (Galaxy 5129)
Dizzy Gillespie / Trumpet Summit Meets The Oscar Peterson Trio (Pablo 2312 114 [OJC 603])

Eddie Harris / Eddie Who? (MCA 33104)
Richard Groove Holmes / Soul Message (Prestige 74329 [OJC 329])
Ahmad Jamal / Chicago Revisited (Telarc 3327)
Ron McCroby / Plays Puccolo (Concord 208)
Helen Merrill / Brownie - Homage to Clifford Brown (Verve 314 522 363)
James Moody / James Moody (Argo 648)
Phineas Newborn / Piano Artistry Of Phineas Newborn (Atlantic 90534)
Phineas Newborn / Tivoli Encounter (Storyville 8221)
Phineas Newborn / World Of Piano (Contemporary 7600 [OJC 175])
Oscar Peterson / London House Sessions (Verve 314 531 766)
Oscar Peterson / Oscar Peterson In Concert (RTE 10022)
Oscar Peterson / Trio (Verve 314 539 063)
Oscar Peterson Trio / At The Concertgebouw (Verve 314 521 649)
Oscar Peterson Trio / Bursting Out / Swinging Brass (Verve 314 529 699)
Emily Remler / Retrospective, vol. 1 Standards (Concord 4453)
Wallace Roney / Munchin' (Muse 5533)
Jackie & Roy / Spring Can Really Hang You Up (DA Music 7609042)
Poncho Sanchez / Fuerte (Concord 340)
Arturo Sandoval / I Remember Clifford (GRP 9668)
Rob Schneiderman / Keepin' In The Groove (Reservoir 144)
Bobby Shew & Vincent DiMartino / Trumpet Summit (Summit 169)
Bob Summers / Joy Spring (Discovery 946)
Bill Warfield Big Band / City Never Sleeps (Sea Breeze Jazz 2048)
Barney Wilen / Talisman (IDA 037)
Anthony Wonsey / Anthonyology (Evidence 22151)

CHILLIN' - Paul Chambers & R. Rachel Mackin
instrumental: WHIMS OF CHAMBERS - Paul Chambers
Paul Chambers / Whims Of Chambers (Blue Note 1534 [Blue Note 37647])
Steve Grossman / Bouncing With Mr. A.T. (Dreyfus 36579)
Steve Grossman / Reflections (Musidisc 500212)
Ron McClure / Never Always (SteepleChase 31355)
Palph Pena / Master Of The Bass (VSOP 97)
Art Pepper / Gettin' Together (Contemporary 47573 [OJC 169])
Wallace Roney / Munchin' (Muse 5533)
Jay Thomas / 360 Degrees (Hep 2060)
Peter Martin Weiss / Bass Hits (Savant 2015)
Rodney Whitaker / Ballads And Blues (Criss Cross 1167)
Dave Young & Phil Dwyer Quartet / Fables And Dreams (Justin Time 53)

THE COASTER - Grachan Moncur III
Kevin Mahogany / Songs And Moments (Enja 8072)
instrumental: THE COASTER - Grachan Moncur III
Curtis Fowlkes / Reflect (Knitting Factory 246)
Bobby Hutcherson / Skyline (Verve 559616)
Grachan Moncur III / Evolution (Blue Note 84153)
John Patton / Soul Connection (Nilva 3406)

CUP OF LIFE - Tom McIntosh & Meredith d'Ambrosio
Meredith d'Ambrosio / Love Is For The Birds (Sunnyside 1101)
instrumental: CUP BEARERS - Tom McIntosh
Kenny Burrell / Midnight At The Village Vanguard (Evidence 22124)
Junior Cook / Place To Be (SteepleChase 31240)
Tommy Flanagan / Confirmation (Enja 4014)
Tommy Flanagan / Eclypso (Inner City IC 3009 [Enja 2088])
Tommy Flanagan / At The Village Vanguard (Blue Note 93155)
Hollyday Brothers / Oh, Brother (Jazzbeat 102)
Dizzy Gillespie / Dizzy For President (Douglas Music 1)
Dizzy Gillespie / Something Old, Something New (Verve 314 558 079)
Benny Golson / Live (Dreyfus 36552)
Peter Leitch / On A Misty Night (Criss Cross 1026)
Joe Magnarelli / Why Not (Criss Cross 1104)
Blue Mitchell / Cup Bearers (Riverside 9439 [OJC 797])

James Moody / Another Bag (Argo LP 695)
James Moody / Moving Forward (BMG/Novus 3026 2 N)
Dado Moroni / Out Of The Night (Jazz Focus 032)
Paul Winter / New Jazz On Campus (Columbia 2064 [Collectables 6686])

DO IT AGAIN - Walter Bolden & R. Rachael Mackin
   instrumental: MR. A.T. REVISITED - Walter Bolden
Art Taylor / Wailin' At The Vanguard (Verve 314 519 677)

DON'T GO - Ralph Moore & Meredith d'Ambrosio
Meredith d'Ambrosio / Love Is For The Birds (Sunnyside 1101)
   instrumental: JOSEPHINE - Ralph Moore
Ralph Moore / Rejuvenate (Criss Cross 1035)
Eastern Rebellion / Mosaic (Music Masters 65073)

EMPTY ROOM - Fritz Pauer & Mark Murphy
   instrumental: SOUND WITHIN AN EMPTY ROOM - Fritz Pauer
Art Farmer & Fritz Pauer / Azure (Soul Note 121126)

FAIR WEATHER - Kenny Dorham
Round Midnight Soundtrack (sung by Chet Baker) (Sony Legacy 85811)
Jeffrey Smith / A Little Sweeter (Verve 314 537 790)
   instrumental: FAIR WEATHER - Kenny Dorham
Dado Moroni / Insights (Jazz Focus 007)
Nicholas Payton / From This Moment (Verve 314 527 073)

FOR OLD TIMES' SAKE - James Williams & Pamela Baskin-Watson
Kevin Mahogany / You Got What It Takes (Enja 9039)
James Williams (sung by I.C.U.) / Truth Justice & The Blues
(Evidence 22142)
   instrumental: OLD TIMES' SAKE - James Williams
Benny Golson / Up Jumped Benny (Arkadia 70741)
James Williams / Magical Trio 1 (EmArcy/Polygram 832 859 2)

FULL MOONLIGHT - Cecil Payne & Rob Bargad
   instrumental: FULL MOONLIGHT AND STARS MADE OF SILVER - Cecil Payne
Cecil Payne / Brooklyn Four Plus One (Progressive 7109)

GARDEN IN THE SAND - Hank Mobley & Bebe Herring
   instrumental: BOSSA DE LUXE - Hank Mobley
Hank Mobley / High Voltage (Blue Note 84273)

THE GIFT OF LOVE - Rodgers Grant
   instrumental: THE GIFT OF LOVE - Rodgers Grant
Sonny Fortune / From Now On (Blue Note 38098)

HEAVENLY! - Jonny King / R. Rachel Mackin
   instrumental: TRYST - Jonny King
Bill Pierce / One For Chuck (Sunnyside 1053D)

HONEYDO - Oscar Brown, Jr.
Oscar Brown, Jr. / Then & Now (Weasel Disc 33342)

I LOVE IT WHEN YOU DANCE THAT WAY - Donald & Dorothy Brown
Donald Brown (sung by Lenora Helm & Eric Walker) / People Music
(Muse 5406)
   instrumental: I LOVE IT WHEN YOU DANCE THAT WAY - Donald Brown
Bill Mobley / Triple Bill (Evidence 22163)
Steve Wilson / Step Lively (Criss Cross 1096)

I'LL REMEMBER LOVE - Milton Sealey & Catherine Whitney
Jeri Brown / Image In The Mirror: The Triptych (Justin Time 151)
   instrumental: THE SETTING SUN - Milton Sealey
Milton Sealey Trio / Windows On The World (Prime Music WOW/WTC)

IN THE MOMENT - Renee Rosnes & Shelly Brown
   FOR THE MOMENT - Renee Rosnes
Renee Rosnes / For The Moment (Blue Note 94859)

IT'S ALL IN THE MIND - Fleurine & Bobby Porcelli
Fleurine / Meant To Be! (Universal 159 085)
   instrumental: REJUVENATE - Bobby Porcelli
T.S. Monk / Charm (Blue Note 89575)
Ralph Moore / Rejuvenate (Criss Cross 1035)
Harris Simon / Short Conversation (Poljazz PSJ 136)

JUST A DREAM - Eddie Higgins & Meredith d'Ambrosio
Meredith d'Ambrosio / Love Is For The Birds (Sunnyside 1101)
   instrumental: FALANDO DE ORLANDO - Eddie Higgins
Warren Vache & Allen Vache / Mrs. Vache's Boys (Nagel-Heyer 050)

JUST A LITTLE DREAMER - Elmo Hope & R. Rachael Mackin
   instrumental: CHIPS - Elmo Hope
Elmo Hope / High Hope! Here's Hope (Classic 16)
Elmo Hope / Trio And Quintet (Blue Note 84438 2)

LIFE'S MOSAIC - Cedar Walton & John & Paula Hackett
T.S. Monk (sung by Miles Griffith) / Higher Ground (Thelonious Records 1009)
Mark Murphy / Some Time Ago (HighNote 7048)
Vanessa Rubin / Pastiche (BMG/Novus 63152)
Diane Witherspoon / You May Never Know (Koch 7879)
   instrumental: MOSAIC - Cedar Walton
Art Blakey & The Jazz Messengers / History Of. . . (Capitol 97190)
Art Blakey & The Jazz Messengers / Mosaic (Blue Note 4090)
Art Blakey & The Jazz Messengers / Three Blind Mice, v. 2 (Blue Note 84452)
Eastern Rebellion / Mosaic (Music Masters 65073)
Stan Getz / Presents Jimmy Rowles: The Peacocks (Sony 52975)
Clifford Jordan / Mosaic (Milestone 47092)
Clifford Jordan / Starting Time (Jazzland J-952 [OJC 147])
Cedar Walton / Art Blakey Legacy (Evidence 22190)
Cedar Walton / Mosaic (Meldac 28102)

LIKE AN OLD SONG - Fritz Pauer & Vanessa Rubin
Cecil Bridgewater (sung by Vanessa Rubin) / Mean What You Say
(Brownstone Recordings 9802)
Cornelia Giese / Rainsong (PG Records 10221)
   instrumental: FAIRYTALE COUNTRYSIDE - Fritz Pauer
Art Farmer / Blame It On My Youth (Contemporary 14042)
Art Farmer / Live At Sweet Basil (Evidence 22104)

LONG AS YOU'RE LIVING - Julian Priester & Tommy Turrentine & Oscar Brown, Jr.
Claudia Acuna / Wind From The South (Verve 543521)
Nancie Banks / Bert's Blues (Consolidated Artists 904)
Jeri Brown / I've Got Your Number (Justin Time 122)
Abbey Lincoln / Abbey Is Blue (Riverside 1153 [OJC 069])
Judy Niemack / Long As You're Living (Free Lance 014)
Max Roach (sung by Abbey Lincoln) / Max Roach & Friends (Jazz View 019)
Roseanna Vitro / Passion Dance (Telarc 83385)
   instrumental: AS LONG AS YOU'RE LIVING - Julian Priester & Tommy Turrentine
Max Roach / Complete Mercury Max Roach +4 Session (Mosaic 201)
Max Roach / Long As You're Living (Enja 4074)
Max Roach / Max Roach And The Turrentine Bros (Jazz View 021)
Tommy Turrentine / Tommy Turrentine (Bainbridge 1047)

LOVE AND DECEPTION - Sergio Mihanovich
Leny Andrade / Leny Andrade (Pointer 203 0008)
Gladys Carbo / So I'll Dream You Again (Consolidated Artists 924)
Sergio Mihanovich / B.A. Jazz (Vik 1080)

Sergio Mihanovich / Sergio Mihanovich (RCA Victor/Sono Radio 393)
Horacio Molina / Horacio Molina (RCA Victor 3539)

LOVE IS FOREVER - Al Grey & Meredith d'Ambrosio
  instumental: AL'S MIST - Al Grey
Al Grey / Trombone By Five (Black & Blue 33.174)
Al Grey & Wild Bill Davis / Keybone (Classic Jazz 103)

THE LOVE WE HAD YESTERDAY - Pamela Baskin-Watson
Betty Carter / It's Not About The Melody (Verve 314 513 870)
  instrumental: THE LOVE WE HAD YESTERDAY - Pamela Baskin-Watson
Bobby Watson / Love Remains (Red 123212)

THE MAN WITH THE MAGIC - Abbey Lincoln & Ronnie Mathews
Abbey Lincoln / People In Me (Verve 314 513 626)
  instrumental: DORIAN - Ronnie Mathews
Roy Haynes / Cracklin' (NJ 8286 [Prestige 818])

MEANT TO BE! - Fleurine & Ray Bryant
Fleurine / Meant To Be! (Universal 159 085)
  instrumental: CHICKEN AN' DUMPLINS - Ray Bryant
Art Blakey & The Jazz Messengers / At The Jazz Corner Of The World
(Blue Note 4016 [Blue Note 28888])
Bobby Timmons / Chicken An' Dumplin's (Prestige 7429)

MOANIN' - Bobby Timmons & Jon Hendricks
Art Blakey (sung by Jon Hendricks) / Buhaina (Prestige 10067
[Prestige 24159])
Double Six Of Paris / Swingin' Singin' (Phillips 600 026 [RCA 65659])
Chris Farlowe / Greatest Hits (Castl 34500702)
Bill Henderson / His Complete Vee Jay Recordings, vol. 1 (Koch 8548)
Lambert, Hendricks and Ross / Hottest New Group In Jazz
(Columbia CL 1403 [Sony C2K 64933])
Judy Niemack / Blue Bop (Freelance CD 009)
Jeffrey Smith / A Little Sweeter (Verve 314 537 790)
Sarah Vaughan / Sarah Sings Soulfully (Roulette 52116 [Blue Note 23517])
various (sung by Jon Hendricks) / The Bebop Singers (Prestige 24216)
  instrumental: MOANIN' - Bobby Timmons
Peter Appleyard / Per-Cus-Sive Jazz (Audiofidelity 7007)
Dick Berk / One By One (Reservoir 143)
Harold Betters / At The Encore (Gateway/RTV Sales 7001)
Harold Betters / Best Of Betters (Spotlite 15115)
Art Blakey / Art Blakey In Europe (RTE 15022)
Art Blakey / Art Of Jazz (In & Out 77028)
Art Blakey & The Jazz Messengers / History Of... (Capitol 97190)
Art Blakey & The Jazz Messengers / Live At Sweet Basil
(GNP/Crescendo 2182)
Art Blakey & The Jazz Messengers / Moanin'
(Blue Note BLP 84003 [Blue Note 46516])
Art Blakey & The Jazz Messengers / Night In Tunisia (Bluebird 63896)
Art Blakey & The Jazz Messengers / Paris, 1958 (Bluebird 7863 61097)
Art Blakey / Hard Bop / Paris Concert (Collectables 5675)
Art Blakey / Jazz Profile, vol. 3 (Blue Note 54899)
Art Blakey / This Is Jazz, vol. 28 (Columbia 65044)
Art Blakey / Wynton Marsalis With Art Blakey, vol. 1 (Jazz Hour 73562)
Ray Bryant / North Of The Border (Label M 495741)
Ray Bryant / Ray Bryant's Tribute (JMI 7503)
Ray Bryant / Solo Flight (Pablo 2310 798 [OJC 885])
Ray Bryant / Through The Years, vol. 1 (Verve 314 512 764)
Ray Charles / Genius+Soul=Jazz / My Kind Of Jazz (Rhino 72814)
James Clay / Cookin' At The Continental (PolyGram/Island 314 510 724)
Contemporary Piano Ensemble / Key Players (DIW 616)
Bill Cosby / Hello Friend (Verve 314 539 171)

John Dankworth / (Big Band International LP 2703 [Columbia B4590])
John DeFrancesco / Hip Cake Walk (HighNote 7071)
Joey DeFrancesco / On The Street Of Dreams (Big Mo 2025)
Joyce DiCamillo / Sunrise Lady (Impulse 8129)
Ron Eschete / Rain Or Shine (Concord 4665)
Art Farmer / Brass Shout (United Artists 4079)
Art Farmer / Plays The Great Jazz Hits (Columbia 2746)
Rosario Giuliani / Live From Virginia Ranch (Philology 114)
Benny Golson / Benny Golson And The Philadelphians (Blue Note 94104)
Benny Golson / In Paris (DRG 8418)
Buddy Guy / Complete Chess Recordings Of . . . (MCA 9337)
Winard Harper / Faith (Savant 2030)
Eddie Harris / Last Concert (Act 9249)
Neal Hefti / Jazz Pops (Reprise R 6039)
Christopher Hollyday / (RBI [Moss Music Group] RBIR 402)
Randy Johnston / Walk On (Muse 5432)
Quincy Jones / Birth Of A Band (Mercury MG 20444 [EmArcy 818 177])
Quincy Jones / Compact Jazz (Verve 832 832)
Quincy Jones / Great Wide World Live (EmArcy/Polygram 822 613 2)
Quincy Jones / Live At The Alhambra 1960 (Jazz Music Yesterday JMY 1004)
Quincy Jones / Live In Goteborg (J-Bop 045)
Quincy Jones / Pure Delight (Polygram Special Projects 20882)
Quincy Jones / Quincy Jones Big Band (Warner Bros 46190)
Junior Mance & Keter Betts & Jackie Williams / FJF Trio (Chiaroscuro 340)
Henry Mancini / Combo (RCA Victor 9026 63192 2) RCA Victor LSP 2258
Herbie Mann / Deep Pocket (Kokopelli Music 1/2)
Herbie Mann / Family Of Mann (Atlantic 1371)
Herbie Mann / Opalescence (Kokopelli 1296)
Billy May / Bill's Bag (Capitol ST 1888 [EMI 35206])
Wes Montgomery / Complete Riverside Recordings (Riverside 4408)
Wes Montgomery / Portrait Of Wes (Riverside 9492 [OJC 144])
Marty Paich / I Get A Boot Out Of You (Warner Bros 1349 [Discovery 962])
Oscar Peterson / Eloquence (Polygram 818 842)
Oscar Peterson / Exclusively For My Friends-Lost Tapes (Verve 529 096)
Oscar Peterson / London House Sessions (Verve 314 531 766)
Oscar Peterson / Trio In Transition (EmArcy/Polygram 405)
Bernard Purdie / Soul To Jazz (Act 9242)
Claudio Roditi / Jazz Turns Samba (Groovin' High 10122)
Philippe Saisse / Next Voyage (Verve 314 537 416)
George Shearing / Complete Capitol Live Recordings (Mosaic 157)
Spirit Of Life Ensemble / Live At the 5 Spot (Rise Up Productions 1008)
Billy Taylor / Uptown (Riverside 1901 [Riverside 1168])
Rene Thomas / Paris 1964 (Royal Jazz RJD 512)
Burnett Thompson / Second Smile (Solace 1002)
Bobby Timmons / From The Bottom (Riverside 3053 [OJC 1032])
Bobby Timmons / This Here Is Bobby Timmons (Riverside 1164 [OJC 104])
Cal Tjader / Verve Jazz Masters, vol. 39 (Verve 314 521 858)
Cal Tjader / Verve Talkin': Roots Of Acid Jazz (Verve 314 527 504)
Cedar Walton / Mosaic (Meldac 28102)

MY LITTLE SHERRI - Charlie Rouse & Ben Sidran
Kevin Mahogany / You Got What It Takes (Enja 9039)
Ben Sidran / Bop City (Antilles 1012)
Ben Sidran / Have You Met . . . Barcelona (Orange Blue 002)
Sidran & McPartland / Piano Jazz (National Public Radio 890617)
  instrumental: LITTLE SHERRI - Charlie Rouse
Charlie Rouse / Moment's Notice (Storyville 8268)
Charlie Rouse & Benny Bailey / Upper Manhattan Jazz Society (Enja 4090)
Charlie Rouse & Stan Tracey / Playin' In The Yard (Steam 116)

NEVER BEEN IN LOVE - Tadd Dameron & Irving Reid
Per Husby (sung by Karin Krog) / If You Could See Me Now (Gemini 89)
Muriel Winston / Fresh Viewpoint (Strata-East 7411)

OH! GEE! - Matthew Gee
Eddie Jefferson / Body And Soul (Prestige 7619 [OJC 396])
Kevin Mahogany / Kevin Mahogany (Warner Bros 46226)
  instrumental: OH! GEE! - Matthew Gee
Eddie Lockjaw Davis / Live at The Widder (Divox 48701)
Eddie Lockjaw Davis / Lock The Fox (Collectables 2812)
Eddie Lockjaw Davis & Johnny Griffin / Blues Up And Down (Jazzland 60
[Milestone 47084])
Duke Ellington / Studio Sessions New York 1962 (LMR 83002) [*G For
Groove* on CD]
Paul Gonsalves & Eddie Lockjaw Davis / Jazz Till Midnight (Storyville 4123)
Tony Graye Quartet & Quintet / Oh! Gee! (Zim 2001)
Johnny Griffin & Lockjaw Davis / Tough Tenors Back Again (Storyville 8298)
Johnny Griffin & Matthew Gee / Soul Groove (Atlantic 1431
[Collectables 6163])
Joe Newman & Henry Red Allen / Hot Trumpets Of Joe Newman
(Swingville 2027 [Prestige 24232])
Ira Sullivan / Horizons (Collectables 6619)

ONE DREAM GONE - Fleurine & Curtis Fuller
Fleurine / Meant To Be! (Universal 159 085)
  instrumental: THE COURT - Curtis Fuller
Curtis Fuller / Boss Of The Soul Stream Trombone (Collectables 6123)
Freddie Hubbard & Miles Davis / Volume 3 (Javelin 03)
various / Super Horns (Warwick 006)

ONE FINE DAY - Ray Bryant & L. Aziza Miller
Tina May / Live In Paris (33 Records 055)
Tina May / One Fine Day (33 Records 050)
  instrumental: CUBANO CHANT - Ray Bryant
Australian Jazz Quintet Plus One / Reunion (AEM Record Group 25801)
Art Blakey / Drum Suite (Columbia (CBS) 1002)
Ray Bryant / Alone At Montreux (Atlantic SD 1626)
Ray Bryant / Con Alma (Columbia CL 1633 [Sony 9519])
Ray Bryant / Lonesome Traveler (Cadet 778)
Ray Bryant / Through The Years, vol. 1 (Verve 314 512 764)
Ron Carter / When Skies Are Grey (Blue Note 30754)
Climax Chicago Blues Band / CCBB Play (Simitar 1402)
El Chicano / Chicano Chant (Universal Music Group 21020)
Essence All Stars / Afro Cubano Chant (Hip Bop Essence 8009)
Wolfgang Dauner / Get Up And Dauner (MPS 533 548)
Martin Denny / Exotic Sounds Of Martin Denny (Capitol 38374)
Harry James / 1964 Live! At The Holiday Inn Ballroom (Jazz Hour 1001)
Jo Jones / Essential Jo Jones (Vanguard 101/02 [Vanguard 8525])
Arthur Lyman / Legend Of Pele (Rykodisc 50432)
Oscar Peterson / Bursting Out – Swinging Brass (Verve 314 529 699)
Oscar Peterson / London House Sessions (Verve 314 531 766)
Oscar Peterson / Peterson Collection (Verve 8271724)
George Shearing / Night Mist (Capitol 943)
Bobby Shew / Salsa Caliente (MMF 1023)
Billy Taylor / Dr T. (GRP 9692)
Art Taylor / Taylor's Wailers (Prestige 7117 [OJC 094])
Cal Tjader / Cal Tjader's Greatest Hits (Fantasy 24736)
Cal Tjader / Latin Concert (Fantasy 8014 [OJC 643])
Cal Tjader / Los Ritmos Calientes (Fantasy 24712)
John Young / Serenata (Delmark 403)

ORANGE BLOSSOMS IN SUMMERTIME - Curtis Lundy & Kurt Elling
Gloria Cooper / Day By Day (GAC Music 1001)
Kurt Elling / Flirting With Twilight (Blue Note 31113)
  instrumental: ORANGE BLOSSOM - Curtis Lundy
Bobby Watson & Curtis Lundy / Beatitudes (Evidence 22178)
Bobby Watson / Jewel (Evidence 22043)

OUR LOVE REMAINS - Robert Watson & Pamela Baskin-Watson
Kevin Mahogany / Double Rainbow (Enja 7097)
  *instrumental: LOVE REMAINS - Robert Watson & Pamela
  Baskin-Watson*
Bobby Watson / Love Remains (Red 123212)
Bobby Watson / Present Tense (Columbia 52400 [Sony 5878])

RHYME OF SPRING - Kenny Dorham & Meredith d'Ambrosio
Meredith d'Ambrosio / Love Is For The Birds (Sunnyside 1101)
  instrumental: POETIC SPRING - Kenny Dorham
Kenny Dorham / Blue Spring (Riverside RLP 1139 [OJC 134])

SEA BREEZE - Jon Burr
  instrumental: SEA BREEZE - Jon Burr
Chet Baker / As Time Goes By (Timeless 251/252)

SOFT AND FURRY - Johnny Griffin & Eddie Jefferson
Eddie Jefferson / Letter From Home (Riverside 9411 [OJC 307])
  instrumental: SOFT AND FURRY - John Griffin
Johnny Griffin / Blues For Harvey (SteepleChase 1004)
Johnny Griffin / Change Of Pace (Riverside 9368 [OJC 1922])
Johnny Griffin / Live In Tokyo (Inner City 60422)
Johnny Griffin / To The Ladies (Galaxy 5139)

SOFT WINDS - Fletcher Henderson & Fred Royal
Mary Stallings / Spectrum (Concord 4689)
Dinah Washington / Bridges Of Madison County (Malpaso 45949)
Dinah Washington / Blue Gardenia (EmArcy 697 124 069
[Jazz Heritage 514 199])
Dinah Washington / Complete on Mercury, v.3 (Mercury 834 675)
Frances Wayne / Warm Sound (Collectables 6626)
  instrumental: SOFT WINDS - Fletcher Henderson
Al Aarons & The L.A. Jazz Caravan (Los Angeles Jazz 001)
Eric Alexander / Alexander The Great (HighNote 7013)
Monty Alexander / Just In Time (Live At EJ's 103.605)
Gene Ammons / Late Hour Special (Prestige 7287 [OJC 942])
Joe Ascione / My Buddy: A Tribute To Buddy Rich (Nagel-Heyer 36)
Georgie Auld / Homage (Xanadu 1226)
Chet Baker / Chet Baker In New York (Riverside 1119 [OJC 207])
Count Basie Meets Oscar Peterson / The Timekeepers
(Pablo 2310 896 [OJC 790])
Rusty Bryant / Rusty Rides Again (HighNote 7074)
Kenny Burrell / All Night Long (Telstar 3603 [Jazz Time 8114])
Kenny Burrell / Night At The Vanguard (Chess 93/6)
Kenny Burrell & Jimmy Smith / Blue Bash! (Verve 314 557 453)
Charlie Christian / Guitar Wizard (Charly LeJazzCD 11)
John Coltrane / Prestige Recordings - Box Set (Prestige 4405)
Concord All Stars (Concord 4172)
John DeFrancesco / Comin' Home (Muse 5531)
Herb Ellis / Nothing But The Blues (Verve 314 521 674)
Ron Eschete / Soft Winds (Concord 4737)
Maynard Ferguson / Complete Roulette Maynard Ferguson (Mosaic 156)
Jimmy Forrest / Most Much! (Prestige 7218 [OJC 350])
Chris Flory / For All We Know (Concord 4403)
Red Garland / High Pressure (Prestige 7209 [OJC 349])
Red Garland / Rediscovered Masters, vol. 2 (Prestige 24078 [OJC 769])
Terry Gibbs, Buddy DeFranco & Herb Ellis / Kings Of Swing
(Contemporary 14067)
Benny Goodman Sextet / Feat. Charlie Christian 1939-41 (Legacy 45144)
Stephane Grapelli / Pent Up House (Drive Archive 41008)
Johnny Griffin & Lockjaw Davis / Tough Tenors (Jazzland 31)
Chico Hamilton Quintet / Complete Pacific Jazz Recordings (Mosaic 175)
Scott Hamilton, Al Cohn & Buddy Tate / Tour De Force (Concord 4172)
Lionel Hampton With Oscar Peterson / Jazz Masters (Verve 314 521 853)

Gene Harris / Down Home Blues (Concord 4785)
Erskine Hawkins / Riff Time (Our World 101072)
Dick Hyman / From The Age Of Swing (Reference Recordings 59)
Illinois Jacquet / Loot To Boot (Delta 7131)
The Jazz Messengers / At The Cafe Bohemia (Blue Note BLP 1507
[Blue Note 46521])
J.J. Johnson & Al Grey / Things Are Getting Better All The Time
(Pablo 2312 141 [OJC 745])
Pete Jolly / Pete Jolly Trio & Friends (VSOP 78)
Barney Kessel / Poll Winners Three! (OJC 692)
Herbie Mann / Live At Newport (Wounded Bird 1413)
Jimmy McGriff / 100% Pure Funk (LRC 30)
Jay McShann / Jimmy Witherspoon & Jay McShann (1201 Music 9031)
Buddy Montgomery / Live At Maybeck Recital Hall, vol. 15 (Concord 4494)
Marty Paich / Jazz Band Ball (Mode 110 [VSOP 23])
Oscar Peterson / At Zardi's (Pablo 2620 118)
Oscar Peterson / Paris Concert (Pablo 2620 112)
Oscar Peterson / Time After Time (Pablo 2310947)
Oscar Peterson & Niels-Henning Orsted Pederson / Digital At Montreux
(Pablo 2308 224 [OJC 383])
Eric Reed / Soldier's Hymn (Candid 79511)
Howard Roberts / All-Time Great Instrumental Hits (Capitol ST 2609
[Euphoria 185])
Joe Roland / Joe Roland (Bethlehem 79856)
Jimmy Smith / Compact Jazz: Plays the Blues (Verve 829 537)
Stuff Smith / Soft Winds (Verve MGV 8206 [Verve 314 521 676])
Art Tatum / Art Tatum Trio (Jazz Anthology 5138)
Art Tatum Trio & Sidney Bechet (Collectables 5613)
The Three Sounds / Good Deal (Blue Note BST 84020 [TOCJ 9167])
various / New Blue Horns (Riverside RLP 294 [OJC 256])

SOMETIME AGO - Sergio Mihanovich
Donna Byrne / It Was Me (Daring 3022)
June Christy / Impromptu (Interplay IP 7710)
Christine Hitt / You'd Be So Nice To Come Home To (MaxJazz 107)
Irene Kral / Kral Space (Catalyst 7625 [Collectables 7160])
Irene Kral / Wonderful Life (Mainstream 56058)
Sandra Mihanovich / Todo Brilla (BMG 60380)
Judy Niemack / About Time (Sony Jazz)
Mark Murphy / Some Time Ago (HighNote 7048)
Carol Sloane / Sweet And Slow (Concord 4564)
Tierney Sutton / Blue In Green (Telarc 83522)
    instrumental: SOMETIME AGO - Sergio Mihanovich
John Abercrombie / Witch Craft (Justin Time 16)
Lori Andrews / Swinging Strings (Jaz Harp 940 3)
Leslie Baker / Askew (Ranch Cabin 1105)
John Basile & Brad Terry / Duo (Music Masters 512744)
Bob Berg / Enter The Spirit (GRP 1105 [Stretch 9004])
Bob Brookmeyer & Friends (Columbia CS 9037 [Sony 65478])
Ray Bryant / Cold Turkey (Sue LP 1032 [Collectables 5749])
Tony Campise / Tony Campise First Takes (Heart Music Inc EATC021CD)
Janusz Carmello / Portrait (Hep 2044)
Bill Evans / You Must Believe In Spring (Warner Bros 3504 [Teldec 835])
Tal Farlow / Return Of Tal Farlow 1969 (Prestige 7732 [OJC 356])
Art Farmer / Interaction (Atlantic SD 1412 [Collectables 6235])
Art Farmer / Meets Mulligan & Hall (Moon 051)
Art Farmer / Quartet 1 (VAP 70474)
Art Farmer & Dizzy Gillespie / Jazz Casual (Koch 8564)
John Hicks & Elise Woods / Single Petal Of A Rose (Mapleshade 02532)
Lee Konitz / Satori (Milestone 9060 [OJC 958])
Steve Kuhn / Years Later (Concord 4554)
Dave MacKay / Windows (MAMA Foundation 1001 2)

Bill Mays & Ed Bickert / Concord Duo Series, vol. 7 (Concord 4626)
Marian McPartland / Just Friends (Concord 4805)
Tete Montoliu Trio / A Tot Jazz 2 (Fresh Sound 49)
Gerry Mulligan / Something Borrowed, Something Blue (Limelight 86040)
Joe Pass / Joy Spring (Blue Note 35222)
Joe Pass / Simplicity (Pacific Jazz 10086)
Niels-Henning Orsted Pedersen / Friends Forever (Milestone 9269)
Michel & Tony Petrucciani / Conversation (Dreyfus 36617)
Lee Ritenour / Stolen Moments (GRP 9615)
Ali Ryerson / In Her Own Sweet Way (Concord 4687)
Akio Sasajima / Time Remembered (Muse 5417)
George Shearing / GAS: Quartet Number Two (Sheba 107)
Clark Terry & Bob Brookmeyer / Terry & Brookmeyer (Mainstream MRL 320)
Clark Terry & Bob Brookmeyer Quintet (Musical Heritage Society 13587)
Ed Thigpen / Mr. Taste (Justin Time 43)
Jack Wilson / Two Sides Of Jack Wilson (EastWest 1154 [Collectables 6177])

STRAIGHT AHEAD - Mal Waldron & Abbey Lincoln
Jeanne Lee & Ran Blake / Newest Sound Around (Jazz! 21122)
Jeanne Lee & Mal Waldron / After Hours (Owl 077 830993)
Abbey Lincoln / Straight Ahead (Candid 8015 [Candid 79015])

SWEET AND TRUE - Curtis Fuller & Catherine Whitney
Gloria Cooper / Day By Day (GAC Music 1001)
    instrumental: SWEETNESS - Curtis Fuller
Benny Golson / One More Mem'ry (Timeless 180)
Kai Winding & Curtis Fuller / Giant Bones 80 (Sonet 834)

THAT MAGIC RAPTURE - Harold Land & Meredith d'Ambrosio
Meredith d'Ambrosio / Love Is For The Birds (Sunnyside 1101)
    instrumental: RAPTURE - Harold Land
Art Farmer / Live At The Stanford Jazz Workshop (Monarch 1013)
Red Holloway / In The Red (HighNote 7022)
Harold Land & Blue Mitchell / Mapenzi (Concord 4044)

THERE'S NO MORE BLUE TIME - Tadd Dameron & Georgie Fame
Per Husby (sung by Georgie Fame) / If You Could See Me Now (Gemini 89)
Mark Murphy / Some Time Ago (HighNote 7048)
    instrumental: A BLUE TIME - Tadd Dameron
Dave Cliff & Geoff Simkins / Play The Music Of Tadd Dameron (Spotlite 560)
Tommy Flanagan / Eclypso (Enja 2088)
Blue Mitchell / Smooth As The Wind (Riverside RLP 9367 [OJC 871])

TWISTED - Wardell Gray & Annie Ross
Lambert, Hendricks & Ross / Hottest New Group In Jazz (Sony 64933)
Jane Monheit / Never Neverland (N-Coded Music 64207)
Mark Murphy / Rah! (Riverside RLP 9395 [OJC 141])
Annie Ross & King Pleasure (sung by Annie Ross) / King Pleasure Sings/
Annie Ross (Prestige RLP 7128 [OJC 217])
Annie Ross / Music Is Forever (DRG 91446)
various (sung by Annie Ross) / The Bebop Singers (Prestige 24216)
various (sung by Annie Ross) / Jumpin' And Jivin' (Specialty 7065)
    instrumental: TWISTED - Wardell Gray
Wardell Gray / Wardell Gray Memorial (Prestige 7008 [OJC 050])

TWO REFLECT AS ONE - Michael Cochrane & Cheryl Pyle
    instrumental: WALTZ NO. 1 - Michael Cochrane
Michael Cochrane / Elements (Soul Note 1151)

THE UNDERDOG - Al Cohn & Dave Frishberg
Meredith d'Ambrosio / It's Your Dance (Sunnyside 1011)
Bob Dorough & Dave Frishberg (sung by Dave Frishberg) / Who's On First?
(Blue Note 23403)
Dave Frishberg / Let's Eat Home (Concord 4402)

Herb Geller (sung by Ruth Price) / Herb Geller Plays The Al Cohn Songbook (Hep 2066)
instrumental: THE UNDERDOG – Al Cohn & Dave Frishberg
Al Grey / New Al Grey Quintet (Chiaroscuro 305)
Turk Mauro / Underdog (Storyville 8265)
Dave McKenna / Giant Strides (Concord 4099)
James Moody / Too Heavy For Words (MPS 15338)

WARM BLUE STREAM – Sara Cassey & Dotty Wayne
Sylvia Copeland / The August Child (Mainstream 56030)
Stan Kenton (sung by Jean Turner) / Some Women I've Known (Creative World ST 1029)
instrumental: WARM BLUE STREAM – Sara Cassey
Nat Adderley / Branching Out (Riverside RLP 285 [OJC 255])
Harry James / Complete Capitol Recordings (Capitol 18720 [Mosaic 192])
Hank Jones / Hanky Panky (Nippon Phonogram/East Wind 4016)
Billy Taylor / Uptown (Riverside RLP 12 319 [OJC 1901])

WE NEVER KISSED – Melba Liston
Gloria Lynne / After Hours (Everest SDBR 1063 [Collectables 5853])

WE'RE ALL THROUGH – Ruby Braff
Ruby Braff (sung by Daryl Sherman) / I Hear Music (Arbors 19244)

WHEN WE MEET AGAIN – Scott Whitfield & Michael Andrew
Manhattan Vocal Project / When We Meet Again (Manhattan Vocal Project CD)

WHEN WE'RE ALONE – Clifford Brown & Michael Stillman
Tuck & Patti / Paradise Found (Windham Hill 11336)
instumental: JOY SPRING – Clifford Brown
Joe Beck / Alto (Digital Music 521)
Boston Brass / Ya Gotta Try (Summit 282)
Anthony Braxton / Piano Quartet Yoshi's 1994 (Music & Arts 849)
Anthony Braxton / Seven Standards 1985, vol. 1 (Magenta MA 0203)
Nick Brignola / Raincheck (Reservoir 108)
Clifford Brown / Jazz Immortal (Pacific Jazz LP 3 [Blue Note 32142])
Clifford Brown & Max Roach (Emarcy 26043 [Verve 543 306])
Gary Burton / New Vibe Man In Town (RCA 52420)
Mike Clark / Give The Drummer Some (Stash 22)
Larry Coryell / Equipoise (Muse 5319)
Buddy DeFranco & Oscar Peterson / Hark (Pablo 2310 915 [OJC 867])
Mark Elf / Mark Elf Trio, vol. 1 (Half Note 00001)
Elaine Elias / Solos & Duets (Blue Note 32053)
Gil Evans / Pacific Standard Time (Blue Note BN LA461 H2)
Gil Evans / There Comes A Time (Bluebird/BMG Music 5783 2 RB)
Stan Getz / Dolphin (Concord 158)
Freddie Hubbard / Born To Be Blue (Pablo 2312 134 [OJC 734])
Freddie Hubbard / Live At Concerts By The Sea (Laserlight 17029)
Barney Kessel / Artistry Of Barney Kessel (Contemporary 021)
Talib Kibwe / Introducing Talib Kibwe (Evidence 22145)
Harold Mabern / Joy Spring (Sackville 2016)
Warne Marsh-Gary Foster Quintet (East World 90024)
Ron McCroby / Ron McCroby Plays Puccolo (Concord 208)
Lanny Morgan / Lanny Morgan Quartet (VSOP 92)
Joe Pass / Joy Spring (Blue Note 35222)
Joe Pass / University Of Akron Concert (Pablo 2308 249)
Joe Pass / Virtuoso #2 (Pablo 2310 788 [Jazz Heritage 13680])
Houston Person & Ron Carter / Something In Common (Muse 5376)
Oscar Peterson / On The Town (Verve 314 543 834)
Oscar Peterson / Plays Jazz Standards (Polygram 833 283)
Oscar Peterson With Stitt, Eldridge & Jones At Newport (Verve MGV 8239)
Oscar Peterson & Gerry Mulligan / At Newport (Verve 8559)
Oscar Peterson & MJQ / . . . At Opera House (Verve 8482)
Oscar Peterson Trio / At The Concertgebouw (Verve 314 521 649)

Tito Puente / Tito's Idea (Sony 81571)
Emily Remler / Retrospective, vol. 1 Standards (Concord 4453)
Arturo Sandoval / I Remember Clifford (GRP 9668)
Doug Sertl / Joy Spring (Stash 565)
George Shearing / Complete Capitol Live Recordings (CEMA 18119)
Bobby Shew / Bobby Shew Metropole Orchestra (Mons 876 821)
Bobby Shew & Chuck Findley / Trumpets No End (Delos 4003)
Bob Summers / Joy Spring A Tribute To Clifford Brown (Discovery 946)
Toots Thielmans / Airegin (Jazz Hour 73526)
McCoy Tyner / Things Ain't What They Used To Be (Blue Note 93598)
U.S. Air Force Airmen Of Note / Children Of The Night (U S Air Force 9103)
Warren Vache / Horn Of Plenty (Muse 5524)
Johnny Varro / Everything I Love (Arbors 19114)

WHO'S BEEN LOVING YOU? – Milton Sealey & L. Aziza Miller
Jeri Brown / Image In The Mirror: The Triptych (Justin Time 151)
instumental: BLUE LOVE – Milton Sealey
Milton Sealey / Windows On The World (Prime Music WOW/WTC)

WHY DO I STILL DREAM OF YOU? – Meredith d'Ambrosio
Meredith d'Ambrosio / Echo Of A Kiss (Sunnyside 1078)

WITHOUT REASON, WITHOUT RHYME – Meredith d'Ambrosio
Meredith d'Ambrosio / Echo Of A Kiss (Sunnyside 1078)

WITHOUT YOU – Renee Rosnes & Shelley Brown
instrumental: MALAGA MOON – Renee Rosnes
J.J. Johnson / Tangence (Verve 314 526 588)
Renee Rosnes / For The Moment (Blue Note 94859)
Renee Rosnes / With A Little Help From My Friends (Blue Note 26584)

YOU ARE MINE – Norman Simmons
instrumental: YOU ARE MINE – Norman Simmons
Norman Simmons / 13th Moon (Milljac 1003)

YOU KNOW WHO! – Bertha Hope
Gloria Cooper / Day By Day (GAC Music 1001)
instrumental: YOU KNOW WHO! – Bertha Hope
Junior Cook / On A Misty Night (SteepleChase 31266)
Bertha Hope / In Search Of . . Hope (SteepleChase 31276)

YOU NEVER MISS THE WATER TILL THE WELL RUNS DRY– Lucky Thompson
Jimmy Scott / Dream (Sire 45629)
Jimmy Scott / Everybody's Somebody's Fool (Coral 60825 [GRP 669])

YOU'LL ALWAYS BE THE ONE I LOVE – Gigi Gryce
Gigi Gryce (sung by Ernestine Anderson) / Nica's Tempo (Savoy MG 12137)

YOU'RE MY ALTER EGO – James Williams & Pamela Baskin-Watson
Mark Murphy / Some Time Ago (HighNote 7048)
James Williams (sung by I.C.U.) / Truth, Justice & The Blues (Evidence 22142)
instrumental: ALTER EGO – James Williams
Donald Byrd / Harlem Blues (Landmark 1516)
Kevin Eubanks / Live at Bradley's (Blue Note 30133)
Roy Hargrove / Vibe (BMG 63132)
Louis Hayes / Quintessential Lou (TCB 99652)
Victor Lewis / Eeeyyess! (Enja 9311)
James Williams / Alter Ego (Sunnyside 1007)

COMPOSER INDEX

LYRICIST INDEX

INSTRUMENTAL TITLE INDEX

Songs by Tempo and Style

suggestions by tempo and genre (style) designed to provide additional performance choices and options when selecting repertoire

The tempo and style markings indicated at the top of each lead sheet represent the composers' original performance concepts. However, the music can often be performed effectively in quite different tempos and styles. For example, upon first considering it, Mark Murphy thought of *You're My Alter Ego* in a medium swing feel, and that's the way he recorded it. It's entirely different from the medium Latin feeling originally envisioned (and recorded) by composer James Williams, but it illustrates that the song can be equally convincing as Latin or swing. Although *Sometime Ago* was conceived as a slow expressive ballad, it has been recorded instrumentally at various tempos, from slow to uptempo swing. The content of the lyric may limit the speed at which you would want to sing the song, of course. A tender love song could very likely not work at a burning tempo.

The combination of music and words creates a new entity, one which can be very different from the music alone. Fleurine was moved by Curtis Fuller's composition *The Court*, but she took it in a very different direction from the way Curtis originally recorded it: as a strong medium up swinger ($\downarrow = ca.$ 230). Fleurine heard the composition as a beautiful ballad *(One Dream Gone)*. Ironically Curtis, upon seeing Fleurine's treatment, revealed that he started writing the composition as a ballad. Obviously, Fleurine's introspective lyric wouldn't work at Curtis's original recorded tempo.

To help you think about the music in this book in a more flexible way, take a look at the following index. A selection may have "medium swing" on the lead sheet; but it could be performed in a faster tempo, making it a "medium up swing." The same is true for ballads, which may also be performed in another tempo or genre. Many songs will be listed under more than one category.

Ballads

Slow Swing

Medium Slow Swing

Sing *JAZZ!* along with a combo or big band

Here's your chance to sing with the band! Some of the songs in *Sing JAZZ!* are also available as combo arrangements or big band arrangements from Second Floor Music. You can visit our website at www.secondfloormusic.com to hear samples of the instrumental arrangements. All the arrangements are supplied with alternate instrumental parts and full scores. These arrangements are in the original instrumental keys indicated below.

Some adjustments will be necessary to have a vocalist sing these arrangements with an ensemble, since the vocal lead sheet may be in a different key than the ensemble arrangement. It's possible for the vocalist to perform the song (with a trio or piano or guitar accompaniment) in his or her own key, then modulate to the ensemble's key for an ensemble entrance.

		arrangement key	product number
All My Love, Especially For You			
Especially For You ..	big band	F	HL00000748
Another Time, Another Place			
Appointment In Milano	quintet	A♭/G	HL00000558
	sextet	A♭/G	HL00000610
Beloved			
Daahoud	quintet	E♭	HL00000742
	septet	E♭	HL00000852
Big Brown Eyes			
Glo's Theme	sextet	F	HL00000967
also in sextet set 2 (6 arrangements)			HL00000941
The Coaster			
The Coaster	sextet	Gm	HL00000620
Do It Again			
Mr. A.T. Revisited	quintet	B♭	HL00000989
also in quintet set 1 (6 arrangements)			HL00000933
Life's Mosaic			
Mosaic	big band	Bm	HL00000794

	arrangement	key	product number

Love Is Forever
Al's Mist	sextet	D	HL00000959
also in sextet set 1 (6 arrangements)			HL00000939

Moanin'
Moanin'	quintet	Fm	HL00000546

One Heart's Dream
Now That The Pain Is Gone sextet		E♭	HL00000969
also in sextet set 2 (6 arrangements)			HL00000941

Our Love Remains
Love Remains	sextet	Gm	HL00000981
also in sextet set 4 (6 arrangements)			HL00000945

Sweet And True
Sweetness	quintet	F	HL00000530
	big band	F	HL00000903

Warm Blue Stream
Warm Blue Stream	quintet	F	HL00000991
also in quintet set 2 (6 arrangements)			HL00000935

When We're Alone
Joy Spring	quintet	F	HL00000550
	septet	E♭	HL00000772

You're My Alter Ego
Alter Ego	quintet/sextet	Am	HL00000608

Typical combo instrumentation for quintets (including alternate parts):
1st part: Trumpet, Alto Sax, C𝄞
2nd part: Tenor Sax, Alto Sax (Baritone Sax), Trombone
Rhythm Section: Piano, Bass, Drums, Guitar

Typical combo instrumentation for sextets (including alternate parts):
1st part: Trumpet, Alto Sax, C𝄞
2nd part: Alto Sax, Tenor Sax
3rd part: Tenor Sax, Baritone Sax, Trombone
Rhythm Section: Piano, Bass, Drums, Guitar

See complete details about the individual arrangements and also hear RealAudio™ clips on our web site, www.secondfloormusic.com, or call 1-800-637-2852 to get a complete catalog. Arrangements are available from your local music dealer.

http://www.secondfloormusic.com

USE OUR WEB SITE TO:

- **hear RealAudio™ clips of each chart**

- **find charts for your group's exact instrumentation**

- **click on any of the fields under SEARCH BY to search for charts. Use the drop-down boxes to fill in the form. *Fill in just the information you're looking for,* like the group size or the level of difficulty you want. Our search engine will compile a list of charts that fit. Click on a title to see details and get the RealAudio icon.**

- **You can also search for charts recorded by some of the great musicians we publish, or the specific instrumentation of your combo.**

- **Try looking for a chart by tempo and group size. Or use the drop-down list under Recording Leader or Recording Title to see what artists have recorded these charts.**

Group Size	1st Part	2nd Part
Quintet	Trumpet	Tenor Sax
3rd Part	**4th Part**	**5th Part**

Arrangement Difficulty	Solo Difficulty
medium	medium

Tempo
uptempo

Recording Leader
JAZZ MESSENGERS

Recording Title

[Submit]   [Clear]

The completed form shown here will display all uptempo quintet charts, medium difficulty, that were recorded by the Jazz Messengers and have a trumpet and tenor sax front line. Select

a title from the results screen and you can hear a short audio clip while you read detailed information about the arrangement, the solo section, the composer and even the recording.

- **browse by composer**

- **browse by composition title**

- **browse by group size: just pick your group size from the drop-down box in the SEARCH BY page**

- **click on a title to see a brief description, including instrumentation, tempo, style, form, solo changes and level of difficulty**

- **click on the RealAudio icon to hear the opening melody**

- **chart descriptions also include brief biographies of our composers**

- **e-mail comments and questions to our staff**

- **request a complete printed catalog**

- **from the HOW TO ORDER page, link to online music dealers and the Hal Leonard Corporation**

- **order our charts from your local music dealer, or order by phone from Music Dispatch at 1-800-637-2852.**

- Use your web browser to visit **http:// www.secondfloormusic.com.** Jazz is our passion—let us show you why!